PETER THE GREAT HUMBLED

The Russo-Ottoman War of 1711

Nicholas Dorrell

'This is the Century of the Soldier', Falvio Testir, Poet, 1641

Helion & Company

Helion & Company Limited
26 Willow Road
Solihull
West Midlands
B91 1UE
England
Tel. 0121 705 3393
Fax 0121 711 4075
Email: info@helion.co.uk
Website: www.helion.co.uk
Twitter: @helionbooks
Visit our blog at http://blog.helion.co.uk/

Published by Helion & Company 2018
Designed and typeset by Serena Jones
Cover designed by Paul Hewitt, Battlefield Design (www.battlefield-design.co.uk)
Printed by Henry Ling Limited, Dorchester, Dorset

Text © Nicholas Dorrell 2017
Images open source unless © individually credited
Colour plate figures by Maksim Borisov © Helion & Company 2017
Maps drawn by George Anderson © Helion & Company 2017

ISBN 978-1-911512-31-8

British Library Cataloguing-in-Publication Data.
A catalogue record for this book is available from the British Library.

For details of other military history titles published by Helion & Company
Limited, contact the above address, or visit our website: http://www.helion.co.uk

We always welcome receiving book proposals from prospective authors.

Contents

List of Illustrations and Maps Within the Text

Acknowledgements

I would like to take this opportunity to thank the many people who have helped me with this project. I would like to thank all at Helion who have helped with the work. The series editor Charles Singleton, George Anderson for the cartography and Maksim Borisov assisted by Boris Megorsky, who created the wonderful artwork. Also many thanks to Boris for his kind support throughout this project. I would also like to mention the continual encouragement of Robert Burke, I hope he finally enjoys the book after waiting so long. Finally I want to thank my family for their patience and support at all times.

Chronology

1686

Russia joins an alliance of nations at war with the Ottoman Empire

1696

The Russians capture the important Ottoman fortress of Azov on the Black Sea

1699 & 1700

The Treaties of Karlowitz and Constantinople end the Russian–Ottoman War of 1686

1709

Charles XII of Sweden is defeated by the Russians at The Battle of Poltava. Charles flees into the Ottoman Empire and initiates a crisis that would lead to the war of 1711.

1710

21 November	The Ottomans, incensed with excessive Russian demands for the surrender of Charles XII, declare war on Russia

1711

Early January	The forces of the Ottomans' ally, the Crimean Khanate, launch an initial short-lived raid on Russian territory
Late January	Tatar armies under Khan Devlet Girey and his son Mehmed Girey launch dual raids on the Ukraine
25–26 March	The Tatars unsuccessfully attack the Russian fortress of Bialocerkiev (White Church)
Late March	Mehmed Girey and Tatars return to the Crimea
10–14 May	The Ottoman army leaves mobilisation area and marches towards the River Danube
Late May	The Russians under General Buturlin and Cossack Hetman Skoropadsky start the delayed attack on the Tatar's Crimea heartland. General Sheremetev leads a Russian advance guard south across the River Dniester towards the Danube
5 June	General Sheremetev's advance guard arrives at the Moldavian capital of Jassy
18–20 June	Main Russian forces cross the River Dnister. The Ottomans cross the Danube and the Tatars join them

28 June	General Renne's detachment from the main Russian army sent to contact the Walachians
2 July	Buturlin and Skoropadsky attack the Crimea with little success. The Tatars counter by moving to cut their lines of supply
7–10 July	The major clash between the Ottomans and Russians on the River Prut ends in disaster and defeat for the Russians
12 July	A peace treaty is signed on the Prut, ending official hostilities
12–14 July	General Renne's Russian flying column, not knowing the war is over, captures the town of Braila, cutting the Ottoman army's supply line
24 July	Buturlin and Skoropadsky retreat from the Crimea without any significant achievements
17 August	After long delays the Russians and their Kalmyk allies under Admiral Apraksin start their successful to attack on the Tatars' Kuban territories
6 September	The Russian forces withdraw from the Kuban, despite a victorious campaign, when news of events on the Prut arrives

1713

24 June	A final peace treaty is signed at Adrianople, formally ending the war

1714

20 September	Charles XII of Sweden leaves the Ottoman Empire and returns home.

Introduction

Interest in the wars of the early part of the eighteenth century seems to be increasing in popularity with the 300th anniversary of events. There is a growing recognition of the importance of this period in the development of standing armies and modern strategy and tactics. The War of the Spanish Succession featuring the exploits of the Duke of Marlborough and Prince Eugene of Savoy is the most celebrated conflict of this era; Eugene's campaigns against the Turks and the Great Northern War between Charles XII of Sweden and Peter the Great of Russia are also relatively famous. However, far less well-known is the Russian–Ottoman War of 1711 which was fought during this period; this war could have easily reversed the outcome of the Great Northern War and changed the future shape of Europe. At the end of the war the Ottomans had the Tsar and Russia at their mercy and could have imposed any conditions they wanted on their defeated opponents, which could have had immeasurable consequences on the course of contemporary and subsequent events. It was obviously, with the benefit of hindsight, a golden opportunity for the Ottoman Empire to halt, or at least slow down, the rise of Russia as a great power. It was the start of the direct confrontation between Russia and the Ottoman Empire which was to be a constant theme of history for the years following these events and played a significant part in the rise of Russia's ascendancy.

Another important aspect of this conflict was Russia's support for the peoples of the Balkans in their desire for freedom from Ottoman domination; although of course this tacit support for independence was not the only motivation for intervention in the region. The war featured sizeable armies made up of diverse national groups, campaigning across huge distances in the three theatres: the Balkans, the Ukraine, and around the shores of the Black Sea. The events of the war continue to have significance for many of the peoples it touched even today. The role of the Danubian princes is part of the national culture of Romania, and Dimitrie Cantemir of Moldavia is still a hero in his own land. The descendants of the Kalmyks still look on this period as a 'golden age' for which they wish a return, and the period marks the time of their nation's greatest extent.

1

The Origins of the War

The underlying reason for the war was the growing tension between the established power of the Ottoman Empire and the rising power of Russia to its north. Before the 1680s the Ottomans viewed Russia as a minor nuisance and would leave their client state the Crimean Khanate, otherwise known as the Tatars, to deal with the Russians while they dealt with more serious problems. During the later seventeenth century, this picture slowly changed as the Russian army began to field growing numbers of western-style regiments and reform their army along the lines of the contemporary armies. This modernisation increased the army's efficiency and the threat it posed, yet despite Russia's growing military might, the Russians had not succeeded in making any significant gains up to this point.

In 1686 this situation changed when the Russians joined a coalition of powers that were fighting the Ottomans at the time. Initially it seemed that once again the Russians would not achieve anything, even though the main Ottoman army was engaged in fighting the other members of the coalition. The early campaigns produced nothing more than growing Russian financial problems and heavy casualty lists despite relatively poor opposition. The largely westernised Russian army could make little headway against the minimal force the Ottomans could bring to face it in the Crimea where the Russians were campaigning. However in 1695 Tsar Peter signalled his growing confidence and stature by personally intervening in the conduct of the war. After initial failure, this led in 1696 to the Russians succeeding in capturing the important Ottoman fortress of Azov on the Black Sea.

With the end of the war Russia secured permanent possession of this important fortress in the subsequent peace treaty. Azov would be an important base for future territorial expansion and gave the Russians access to the Black Sea. The Tsar immediately started constructing a Russian Black Sea fleet at the nearby port of Taganrog, clearly signalling his intention to expand Russian influence and territory in this area. This was an obvious threat to the Tatars and they were further implications for them as in addition Russia secured important concessions concerning the Tatars of the Crimean Khanate. Before this time the Russians had been too weak to prevent the Tatars from regularly raiding Russian territory or extorting tribute to halt their attacks. In most years the Tatars had taken a heavy tribute from the

Russians in one form or another. The Treaty of Karlowitz put an end to this 'traditional' Tatar practice, much to the disgust of the Tatars themselves.

It was not only the Crimean Tatars who were displeased by the treaty. The Ottomans felt they had been forced into concessions by the activities of the other members of the coalition more than by the Russians. There was a lingering feeling that the Russians did not deserve the rewards they had gained. The Ottomans and Tatars thought that despite the successes in the recent war the Russian army was still not a credible force and could be easily beaten if fighting alone. The Russian success in the war was because the bulk of the Ottoman and allied forces were engaged with the other members of the coalition the Russians belonged to. Yet given time the threat from the Russians would clearly grow, and indeed it had at the time, so action was needed soon to reverse the trend. Powerful factions within the Ottoman Empire and the Crimean Khanate were therefore anxious to reverse Russia's 'unmerited' gains and destroy the growing threat that Russia represented.

The shift in fortunes created by the terms of the Treaty of Karlowitz also changed the situation for the enemies of the Ottoman. It was obvious that the Russians would seek to exploit their newly acquired base on the Black Sea in the near future. The fleet they were building was a clear indication of ambitious plans for further expansion, and the Russians had potential allies in the area that would be willing to help. The Kalmyks were an independent Khanate established when the group migrated into the area in the early seventeenth century. They were at the height of their power at this time and it is considered to be their 'golden era'. Ayuka Khan had a strong relationship with the Russians and was eager to benefit from their alliance, expanding their territory and influence primarily at the expense of their Muslim neighbours. Similarly the majority of the Cossacks could also be counted on for support in future attacks on their traditional Tatar and Ottoman enemies. Many of the Cossacks had proved to be reluctant allies of the Russians in the years before this conflict. Sections of all of the main Cossack groups had revolted against the Russians – usually in support of the Swedes – in the years before 1711. A Russian attack on their common Ottoman and Tatar enemies would therefore be useful in improving ties with the Cossacks, as the Cossacks could be relied on to unite against their traditional foes. While war could bind the Cossacks more closely to the Russians, it could also possibly open the way for Russians to acquire new client states and allies. Moldavia and Walachia were two Christian states under the dominion of the Ottomans and within reach of Russian-controlled territory. These states dreamed of escaping from Ottoman rule and they hoped with Russian help this could be accomplished. Both states were very nervous about the risks involved but having a powerful ally like the Russians might make it possible to achieve their dream. Secret negotiations had been proceeding between them and the Russians following the treaty of 1699, but after 1709 these talks became more urgent.

The event in 1709 which transformed the situation was the defeat of the Swedish Army at Poltava. The Swedes had been campaigning against the Russian Empire since 1700 and had invaded Russia in 1708, but the invasion ended in disaster at Poltava in the Ukraine. Charles XII of Sweden and the pitiful remnants of his army escaped into the Ottoman Empire. At first King Charles was treated as an honoured guest by the Sultan and set up a court

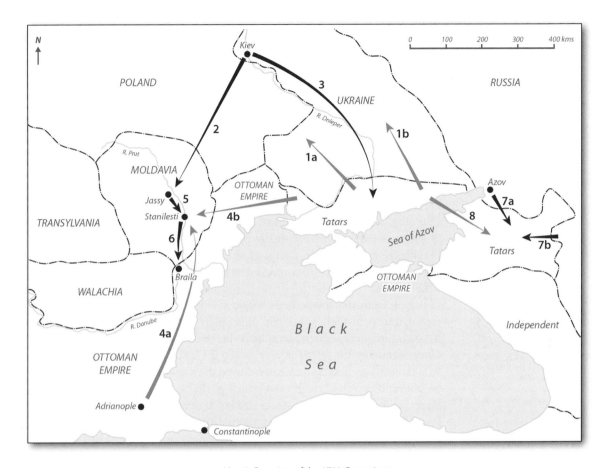

Map 1. Overview of the 1711 Campaigns

1: Tatar Raids (January to April) – 1a Mehment Girey – 1b Khan Devlet Girey II

2: The main Russian army under Tsar Peter moves into Moldavia and joins its Moldavian allies (May–June)

3: An army of Cossacks with Russian support under Skoropadsky attack the Crimea area defended by Devley and Bahti Girey (May–July)

4: The Ottoman army and its allies move into Moldavia (May–July)

4a: The Ottoman army under Baldaci Mehmed assembles and advances north

4b: After the Tatar raids Mehmed Girey leads a strong allied contingent to join the Ottoman army

5: The Russian main army meets the Ottoman army at Stanilesti near the River Prut (Early July)

6: Renne's Russian flying column detached from the main army captures Braila but is then forced to surrender (July)

7: Pro-Russian forces launch a delayed attack on the Kuban area (August–September):

7a: Apraksin with a force of Russians and Cossacks open the attack

7b: Kalmyk reinforcements under Khan Ayuka arrive

8: Bahti Girey with a force of Tatars and Cossacks goes to aid the Kuban forces in exile at Bender. The Swedish exiles were joined by other exiles following the disastrous 1709 campaign. These were Cossacks who had fought on the Swedish side in the Russian campaign or revolted against the Russians, and also Polish supporters of the Swedish candidate for the Polish throne whose position also collapsed after Poltava. Not unnaturally the Russians requested that the Ottomans surrender Charles and the exiles or at least expel him from their territory. This would give them the opportunity to finish the war with Sweden quickly. With Charles' arrival in Ottoman territory the hawks in the Ottoman leadership were greatly strengthened by the various exile groups. The hawks now perceived an opportunity to act in their own interests and were not slow to exploit it. The Ottomans were undecided whether to comply with Russian demands and the court became the centre of frenzied intrigue. Partisans of different camps argued their case, large sums of money probably changing hands behind the scenes, but the situation remained unresolved.

Most of this activity eventually centred on a scheme for Charles XII and his allies to be escorted by a large group of Ottoman and Tatar soldiers across Poland to the territory still controlled by the Swedes in Northern Germany. The details of these schemes varied over time but usually involved tens of thousands of troops. In theory the perhaps 50,000-strong escort of Ottomans and Tatars would return to their homeland after safely escorting the Swedish king to his own territory, perhaps along with the 10,000 plus fellow exiles at Bender. Understandably, the Russians, and indeed the Poles, doubted that they actually would return home after they had escorted the King or that their passage would be uneventful. While clearly the return of the Swedish king, possibly with a large contingent of allied Cossacks and Poles, was also not an attractive option. Instead, the Russians kept pushing alternatives but grew increasingly frustrated with the progress of the talks. In the negotiations it was assumed that all parties would agree to the scheme but there was also the possibility – unspoken, but troubling for the Russians – that the Ottomans would act unilaterally. The Russian Tsar eventually made war inevitable as Peter progressively made more strident demands for the Ottomans to relinquish the fugitive Swedish king. Perhaps this was because of frustration at Ottoman inertia, perhaps because of fears that the Ottomans would escort the Swedish king across Poland without agreement, perhaps because of overconfidence after recent military successes and diplomatic developments. Which ever was the case the Russian demands were the final *casus belli*. The Ottomans, increasingly offended at the aggressive nature of these demands, refused to submit. The Tsar was clearly in no mood to wait for compliance and the Ottomans, in a final act of stubborn rejection, declared war on 21 November 1710. This was too late in the year to start campaigning and so both sides started preparations for active warfare in 1711.

The campaign would unfold over a wide area and can be divided into two main theatres. The main theatre was the Russian invasion of the Balkans by the main Russian army, which was opposed by the Ottoman army. The other theatre of operations was in and around the Tatar lands. These included Tatar raids into Russian controlled Ukraine and campaigning in the Crimea and Kuban areas. In these actions the Russian forces were usually a minority of an army consisting largely of allied troops. These battled against opposing forces largely composed of the Ottomans' Tatar allies.

2

The Opposing Commanders

The Russians and their Allies

Tsar Peter I (the Great) of Russia (1672–1725)

Tsar Peter was a great leader of Russia who earned the title 'the Great' for his achievements. He is widely credited with transforming Russia into a modern state. After a troubled childhood and period when he shared the throne, Peter became the sole ruler of Russia in 1694. At this time Russia ad its allies were already in an ongoing war with the Ottomans and their allies. In this war he eventually achieved success with the capture of the important fortress on the Black Sea of Azov, which was confirmed in the treaty of Karlowitz. In 1700 he led Russia into the major event of his reign and a formative event in Russian history, the Great Northern War. This war with Sweden was to establish Russia as the dominant force in the area and as a great power. During the war Peter set about founding a Russian navy, modernising the Russian army, state and culture. Initially Russian forces had struggled in the war but their victory at Poltava in 1709 destroyed the Swedes as a serious threat. However while the Swedish king remained at liberty in exile in the Ottoman Empire he showed no inclination to end the war between Sweden and Russia. There was still a chance that the exile could reverse Sweden's fortunes somehow, and he saw a opportunity to do this with Ottoman help. In 1711 Peter would in frustration lead the main Russian army in a campaign to force the issue and nearly lose everything in the process. The campaign ended with Peter and his army at the mercy of the Ottomans, a situation he was lucky to escape from cheaply. Despite this setback he went on to win the war against Sweden after 10 more years of campaigning. He established Russia as a 'Great Power', a position it holds to this day.

Count Boris Sheremetev (1652–1719)

Sheremetev was the most experienced Russian general of the time, and the commander-in-chief of the army. An officer in the army since 1681, he was in command of the cavalry at the disastrous Battle of Narva in 1700 and became commander of the main Russian army after the battle. In the following years Sheremetev had mixed fortunes but slowly reduced Swedish control of the Baltic provinces of their Empire. In 1705 and 1706 he campaigned in Poland

and emerged as the undisputed Russian senior commander. During the decisive Russian campaign of 1708 and 1709 he was nominally in charge of the main Russian army. During all this time it is often difficult to separate his contribution to events; sometimes he operated on his own but on other occasions Tsar Peter was also with his army. In theory Peter was not in charge of the army but instead acted in some junior capacity, but of course he was still Tsar and so it is difficult to tell the exact role of the two in decisions made. Whatever the case, it is clear that Sheremetev was a key advisor to Tsar Peter and the most important Russian commander of the time. He was the first person to ever be appointed a Russian Count, which is a clear indication of his value to Peter the Great. In 1711 Peter once again relied on Sheremetev's skills to help command the main Russian army.

1. Tsar Peter the Great

Hetman Ivan Skoropadsky of the Ukrainian Cossacks (1646–1722)

In 1708 as part of the Great Northern War, the Swedes invaded the Ukraine, Skoropadsky was the colonel of a Ukrainian Cossack regiment. At this time the Ukrainian Cossacks were allied to the Russians, but Mazeppa, the reigning Hetman, was unhappy with the alliance and planned to switch sides and join the Swedes. Unfortunately for Mazeppa his scheme was overtaken by events and the planned coup only half succeeded. Mazeppa and a part of the Ukrainian Cossack army joined the Swedes but many did not. Skoropadsky was ideally placed to seize control of the pro-Russian faction within the Ukrainian Cossacks and support the Russians. This he did and was awarded the Ukrainian Hetmanship in place of Mazeppa by the grateful Russian Tsar. He fought the rest of the Russian campaign (1708–09) as head of the Ukrainian Cossacks. However his position was still weak, as the Tsar did not fully trust him and neither did many of his own people; the divisions of the attempted switch of sides remained unhealed. He was to lead the mainly Cossack forces that were to attack their traditional Tatar enemies in the Crimea. He hoped that success there would improve his standing among the Cossacks and gain their full support.

Khan Ayuka of the Kalmyk Khanate (1669–1724)

The Kalmyk Khanate was to the south of the Russian border at the time, and the Khan was a reliable Russian ally. The Kalmyks were relative newcomers to the area and seeking to secure their position in a hostile environment. The Kalmyks protected the Russians' southern frontier and helped with their conflicts in the area, and at the same time the Russians provided support against the Khan's enemies in Central Asia and the Caucasus. Ayuka, the reigning Khan, maintained this successful relationship loyally. This led to the Khanate reaching a zenith in terms of economic, military, and political power, a time that is considered a golden era. In 1711 the Khan would lead his forces in an attack on the Tatar-controlled Kuban area in cooperation with the Russian commander Apraksin.

Count Fyodor Apraksin (1661–1728)

Apraksin had been a friend to the Tsar since Peter's childhood and during his youth had built him a toy flotilla of ships. When Peter finally gained full control of Russia it was natural for the Tsar to give his friend greater responsibilities. He was the third ever Russian to be appointed Count. Apraksin acted as a field commander of the army but was also one of Russia's first admirals. For a long time he combined the two roles and was responsible for building Russia's new Baltic navy and commanding the army that protected the growing Russian Baltic fleet and its base at St Petersburg. He was a competent and trusted commander but nothing more. Therefore he was often given independent command of important, but secondary, tasks. Apraksin was given command of the Russian task force that was to help Russia's allies attack the Kuban area of the Tatar territories.

Above: 2. Count Boris Sheremetev, commander-in-chief of the Russian army.

Below: 3. Dimitrie Cantemir, *voivode* of Moldavia

Voivode (Prince) Dimitrie Cantemir of Moldavia (1673–1723)

Born into the Moldavian royal family in 1673, Dimitrie Cantemir was only nominally Voivode of Moldavia for long periods. The country was an Ottoman satellite state and the Ottomans retained the final word on internal policy. The Ottomans decreed that until 1710 the country was ruled by a relative of the Walachian *hospodar* Constantine Brâncovan. This would cause a lot of mistrust between the two leaders during the crucial period of 1710–1711 when Cantemir was finally in command in Moldavia. In 1710 the Ottomans replaced the existing leader of Moldavia with Cantemir because they feared that the former ruler was plotting with the Russians and other enemies of the empire. This was ironic, as Dimitrie Cantemir quickly became disillusioned with empty Ottoman promises and proved to be far more pro-Russian than his predecessor. In 1711 Cantemir led his army to join the Russians and support the campaign as much as he could. Unfortunately for Cantemir the campaign resulted in defeat, and could have led to him being handed over to the Ottomans. Only Tsar Peter's standing by his ally saved him from this fate and he was

DEMETRIVS CANTEMIR. S.ROSSIACI IMPERII, et MOLDAVIÆ. PRINCEPS. PETRI.M.RUSSORU *Imperatoris* SENATOR.et AB IN TIMIS CONSILIIS

able to escape into exile. After the campaign Cantemir proved that he had a true gift as a linguist, history, philosopher, musician, etc., and in exile he built up a reputation as a Renaissance man which continues to this day. This artistic ability combined with his attempt to establish an independent state has meant that he remains a national hero.

The Ottomans and their Allies

Sultan Ahmed III (1673–1736)

4. Ottoman Sultan Ahmed III

Ahmed III ascended the Ottoman throne in 1703 after the abdication of his brother, Mustafa II. His brother had been Sultan during a period that the Empire's power had begun to decline. Mustafa II had sought radical changes to reverse this trend, but had failed and was forced to abdicate. Like all Sultans had for some time, Ahmed did not usually undertake active responsibility for government or campaigning in the field. The Grand Vizier was the head of the Ottoman government and the day-to-day running of the empire, including being in charge of leading the army and pursuing imperial policy. Ahmed was reluctant to fight the Russians but was forced into the war against his wishes. As events turned out the 1711 campaign offered an opportunity to reverse the trend of history, a chance that was not taken, though of course this is perhaps more obvious with hindsight than it was at the time. What is clear is that Ahmed presided over a relatively prosperous period for the Ottoman Empire. The Empire regained some of the land lost in the previous reign and indeed made some territorial gains, and Ahmed also oversaw some important changes in its finances. Unfortunately in the long term these would not prove to be enough to save the Ottomans; the Empire was not yet declining but it was perhaps stagnating.

Grand Vizier Baldaci Mehmed Pasha (1662–1712)

Baldaci Mehmed was the Grand Vizier at the time of the 1711 campaign. The Grand Vizier was a key role within the Empire being commander of the army, chief minister of the government and effectively in control of the administration. The power of the position meant competition for the post was, often literally, cut-throat. The office of Grand Vizier was surrounded by intrigue, bribery and worse. Different factions within the higher echelons of Ottoman society vied for this power and many Grand Viziers did not rule for long. The time of the 1711 campaign was Baldaci Mehmed's second period of office: the first was from December 1704 to May 1706. This second spell in office lasted from August 1710 and would finish in November 1711 after the campaign had finished. Baldaci Mehmed had no military experience and showed little military ability during the campaign. Poniatowski said he had never seen an army before the campaign and was by nature a poltroon who believed he would always lose if attacked.[1] Despite this, Baldaci Mehmed directed the day-to-day running of the war and led the main Ottoman Army. Under his direction the Ottomans succeeded in forcing the surrender of the Russian Tsar and all his troops. Unfortunately, he was also responsible for letting this valuable opportunity pass and for the excessively lenient terms imposed. It is often speculated that this may have been the result of a large Russian bribe. This may be true, as there are stories about the wives of the Russians in the camp collecting jewels and money for bribes. Given the volatility of Ottoman internal politics, Baldaci Mehmed would not be the first to put personal gain before the needs of the state.

Khan Devlet Girey II of the Crimean Khanate (1654–1725)

Devlet was a member of the Girey dynasty that had ruled the Crimean Khanate, often called the Tatars, since 1441. At this time the Tatars were a satellite state of the Ottoman Empire, but because of their military power the relationship was more equal than in other such relationships. The Tatars too were under increasing pressure from surrounding powers and struggling to maintain their former elevated position. They were one of the main advocates of war with Russia and in particular resented the terms of the Treaty of Karlowitz 1699. This greatly restricted their raiding activities, while the Russian occupation of Azov and surrounding area along with their shipbuilding activites were a direct threat to them. Devlet Girey succeeded to the Khanate in 1699 when his father retired to go on a pilgrimage, but in 1702 he stepped down again in favour of his father who returned to power. In 1709 he once again assumed the throne and was immediately plunged into the intrigue surrounding the arrival of Charles XII of Sweden. Devlet Girey was one of the main leaders of the hawks within the Ottoman elite and strongly supported the war with Russia. He was commander-in-chief of the forces defending the Khanate and concentrated on defending the Crimea area during the fighting.

Devlet Girey's sons Bahti and Mehmed Girey

These sons of Devlet Girey played a prominent role in the events of the campaign, acting as the field commanders of the Khanate's forces. After the initial raid, the brothers had divided responsibility. Bahti initially commanded the Tatar forces on the left bank of the River Dnieper in the main raid. Afterwards he commanded the forces that remained in the Crimea to successfully defend the homeland from attacks by the mainly Cossack armies sent to attack them. Once the attack on the Kuban area by the Russians and their allies developed, Bahti Girey moved to this area to lead the local forces defending it. He successfully halted the invasion of Tatar land in the Kuban and drove the invaders back into Russian territory. Mehmed Girey was initially in charge of the Khanate and allied forces on the right bank of the Dnieper. After the raid he led the main Tatar army and allied force which joined the main Ottoman army to oppose the main Russian force in the Prut area. Mehmed Girey commanded the Tatar forces which helped force the Tsar's army to surrender.

---

1   S. Poniatowski., *Remarks on M. de Voltaire's History of Charles XII, King of Sweden*, 1761, p. 59.

5. Hospodar (Prince) Constantine Brâncoveanu of Walachia

Hospodar (Prince) Constantine Brâncoveanu of Walachia (1654–1714)

Constantine Brâncoveanu rose to power in Walachia after the 'mysterious' death of the former ruler. He arranged the exile of his uncle and nephew who were also his chief rivals and became *hospodar* in 1689. He instituted an architectural style which was named after him. He meddled in the affairs of Walachia's neighbours, including Moldavia, which brought him into dispute with Dimitrie Cantemir of Moldavia. The acrimonious rivalry this caused would make cooperation between the two very difficult during the following campaign. Walachia, and its neighbour, was a satellite state of the Ottoman empire. He sought outside aid for his plans to make Walachia independent from its Ottoman overlords, and so as the growing crisis surrounding the arrival of the Swedish king in the region developed, he secretly contacted the Russians and negotiated an alliance. In spite of this scheming he was still reluctant to openly show his hand because of his fear of reprisals. Because of this he prevaricated during much of the campaign and hung back from actually aiding the Russians. With the arrival of the main Ottoman army in the vicinity of Walachia he half-heartedly chose to side with them. In spite of his support the Ottomans were suspicious of his actions during the campaign. After the war Brâncoveanu was arrested and executed by them.

King Charles XII of Sweden (1682–1718)

Charles XII succeeded to the Swedish throne in 1697 following the death of his father. His youth and inexperience encouraged a hostile alliance of Denmark, Norway, Saxony, Poland-Lithuania and Russia to attack Sweden, and war broke out in 1700. A successful attack on Denmark was followed by a long, but equally victorious campaign in Poland and an invasion of Saxony – this only left Russia as a Swedish enemy by 1707. In 1708 Charles led the Swedish army into Russia to knock this last opponent out of the war, but instead it was Tsar Peter who emerged victorious as the Swedish army was crushed at Poltava in the summer of 1709. Fleeing from the battle with only a small escort of Swedish troops Charles entered Ottoman territory where his Russian pursuers could not follow. The Ottomans initially gave the exiled Charles a warm welcome. His arrival exasperated an already tense situation in the area and he schemed to try to use the power of the Ottomans to his advantage. His arrival in Ottoman territory also strengthened the hawks in the Ottoman court. This scheming, and his presence, were the sparks that ignited the war of 1711. Charles remained inside Ottoman territory and continued scheming, with diminishing effect, until 1714 when he finally admitted it would not work. Travelling with a small entourage he returned to Swedish territory to resume the war with Russia. By the time he returned to his homeland the situation for Sweden was dire. Still campaigning to save the situation for Sweden, Charles was killed in 1718 in operations in Norway.

3

The Opposing Armies

The armies fielded by both sides were recruited from diverse sources, and this section will briefly describe their organisation and appearance. Many of the troops engaged in the war were irregular forces or are very poorly documented, at least in English. This means that unfortunately details are often lacking and only a general picture can be given. It is therefore important to remember that in practice for most of the different forces involved there would be a great deal of variety in dress and equipment.

The Russians and their Allies

The Russian Army

When Peter first became Tsar, the Russian army was still a hybrid army composed of the old-style units of the earlier seventeenth century and the new-style units similar to those used by most the rest of Europe. By 1711 the Russian army had largely been remodelled along contemporary western lines. Some older-style units such as the *streltsi* did exist, but were generally only used for garrison and other supporting duties. However, some of these troops would have seen active service defending against the initial Tatar raids and a few were involved in the Crimean and Kuban offensives. Despite this, the bulk of the Russian forces generally, and all the regiments involved in the Balkans campaign, were of the new style and have been identified. The exact make up of units on the secondary fronts is not known, and there does not appear to be enough of the most up-to-date new-style regiments unaccounted for to account for all the troops used. Therefore it is likely that some of the units on these fronts, particularly the infantry, were of the older style. There were still some units of *streltsi* infantry and Horse Service cavalry units active in the area. These were old Russian-style regular units which had been part of the army for a long time but had been steadily replaced by Western-style units in the years before 1711. The horse service units were largely replaced by Western-style dragoon units after the poor performance of these units in the early part of the Great Northern War. The *streltsi* had been supplemented by, and progressively replaced by, Western-style infantry units for decades before this period. This process was accelerated in the early stages of the Great Northern War. Initially the new Western-style units were

6. Von der Ropp Horse Grenadiers in the 1711 campaign. Illustration by Adlophe Charlemagne (1826–1901), from the regimental history of the 13th Ordensky Dragoons (1912).

known as Colonel XXX's regiment, where XXX was the current colonel's name. The unit's name would thus change when it had a new colonel. As the Great Northern War progressed the best of the Western-style units were 'named'. They received a permanent name, usually that of a province or something similar. From this time the 'named' units became the normal units used in frontline activities while the others that remained, 'Colonel XXX's regiment, were relegated to garrison and other supporting activities.

There were 38 infantry and 30 cavalry regiments fighting on the three fronts during the Russian sponsored offensives. Others were involved in the defensive actions against the Tatar raids in the early part of the campaign and generally on garrison and similar duties. There were 20 'named' cavalry units and 34 'named' infantry regiments with 75 battalions involved with the operations of the main army in the Balkans. The cavalry in this theatre consisted of three horse grenadier regiments, 16 line dragoon regiments and one dragoon squadron. While the infantry contingent was two guard regiments with a total of seven battalions, four grenadier regiments with a total of eight battalions and 28 line regiments with a total of 60 battalions. Of the line infantry, two regiments consisting of seven battalions were veterans of long standing and considered 'elite' units. There were 122 guns of various kinds with the main army when it surrendered, and there were up to 20 guns with the cavalry flying column detached from this force at the time. Therefore the army probably had over 140 artillery pieces in total. A further four infantry regiments and 10 dragoon regiments operated in support of allied offensive operations. In addition there were an unknown number of others who were doing garrison and other similar duties. Both the units supporting the allied offensive operations and those performing other duties

Above: 7. Pistols of the Russian army. Exhibition of Artillery Museum, St. Petersburg.
Below: 8. Hilt of a broadsword found on Poltava battlefield. Exhibition of Azov Museum.
(Both from the collection of Boris Megorsky)

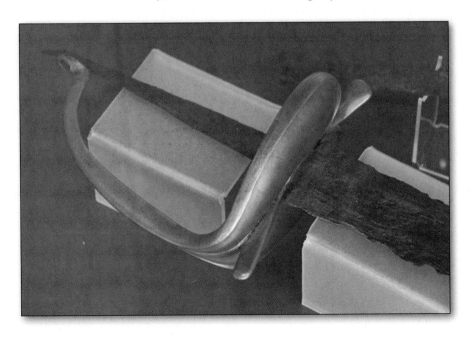

9. Western-style Russian infantry. Reenactment group 'Preobrazhensky Life Guard Regiment, 1709'. (From the collection of Boris Megorsky)

were probably old-style Russian units or Western-style units which had not been 'named', i.e. lower class units to those in the main field army.

The Russian Infantry

Russian infantry was organised into battalions with a nominal strength of 700 to 750 men in four companies. Normally the battalions would rarely achieve this strength in practice. However there was an effort to recruit the units involved in this campaign to as near as possible to this strength and so it seems likely that they were around this size at the start of the campaign. Even if something like full strength was achieved, the units would have quickly dwindled in size through sickness, desertion and normal campaign attrition. This was particularly true as the troops all made long marches during the campaign and often under difficult conditions. There were a few units in the army which only had a single battalion but the vast majority were in regiments of two battalions; at least five of the regiments involved in the campaign had three battalions, and one regiment had four.

Western-style Russian infantry were dressed and equipped in the standard manner of the period. The uniform generally consisted of a long coat with cuffs but no turnbacks, waistcoat, breeches, stocking and a tricorn hat. Some units wore a Russian hat called a *karpus* which was a coloured felt hat, often with a lining of a different colour. This second colour showed when the cap was worn, as the edge was turned up. A third type of headwear was also worn, the grenadier cap: this was of the mitre type and is generally considered to have been in two colours. Evidence for the colours of these caps at this time is scarce and the colours given in many sources actually date from a later period. *Streltsi* wore a long kaftan-style coat with a hat with fur around the bottom.

The troops were equipped with a flintlock musket, small sword and bayonet; grenadiers could also be armed with grenades. Usually one in eight of the soldiers within a battalion, except grenadier units, was armed with a pike. However, in 1711 the regular battalions in the main army left their pikes in storage and it is likely that the other battalions did the same. Instead, for this campaign, the Russians would rely on stakes and other similar defences carried by individual soldiers and various other portable defences carried in the baggage, to deter cavalry attack. The Imperialist armies had taken a similar approach in their campaign against the Ottomans in the 1690s.[1] Some of the Russian senior officers had participated in or observed these campaigns and clearly this experience influenced aspects of this campaign. The Imperialists had also discarded their pikes and used various portable defences instead, which they placed before the unit when an attack seemed imminent. The Tsar ordered that one in five of the infantry should have sharpened wooden stakes. These along with other *rogatki*, a term meaning a variety of similar devices like *chevaux-de-fries*, would be used to help resist the furious Ottoman attacks expected. Like the Russians, the Imperialists normally used a form of rank firing in combat. Yet when fighting the Ottomans they switched to a form of continuous firing similar to the platoon firing used by other armies of the period. In the earlier campaign the Imperialists used these two measures to stop the nimble Ottoman forces taking advantage of their skills. It is not known if the Russians also changed their firing system, but they had a similar system and logically it would seem appropriate to use it. The Russians usually fought in four ranks at this time, often with the front rank being held in reserve.

Table 1 presents uniform information that is known for the infantry involved in the 1711 campaign. Wherever possible uniform details are contemporary to the period or the best available from before the campaign, but where no details are available the entry has been left blank. Where it seems possible that the uniform details from an earlier period would still apply a date has been included after the information. For example in the table the Ingermanlandski regiment has white hat lace in 1703 and there is no description of a later hat edging, so it may still have been the same in 1711. In other listings an alternative colour is given in brackets, and in this case the evidence is not clear and both alternatives are equally as likely.

---

1   R. Hall and G. Boeri, *Uniforms and Flags of the Imperial Austrian Army 1683–1720* (Pike and Shot Society, 2009), p. 134..

The Russian Cavalry

Russian cavalry was organised into companies with a nominal strength of about 100–120 men. Most units were organised into regiments and had 10 companies, but a smaller number of units were called 'squadrons' and only had five companies. Regiments with the addition of the regimental staff were around 1,200 to 1,300 men at full strength, with 'squadrons' being about half this size. It was of course rare for a unit to be up to full strength and they would quickly dwindle once active campaigning began. Yet once again it seems that an effort was made to bring the units up to full strength at the start of the campaign.

As with the infantry, the cavalry were armed and dressed in a similar manner to Western troops of the same period. Most Russian cavalry regiments were dragoons but they also had three regiments of horse grenadiers. These units used standard Western cavalry tactics but they also used other tactics not common at the time. They frequently dismounted to fight on foot and also operated alongside infantry mounted on separate horses or 'two up' on a cavalryman's horse. These tactics were used in other armies but only occasionally. In contrast they were common in the Russian service. Standard uniforms were in the same style as the infantry uniform with the addition of cavalry boots. The dragoons wore a uniform similar to that worn by the line infantry while the horse grenadiers wore one similar to the grenadiers. Like the infantry, the dragoons could wear the *karpus* instead of the more familiar tricorn. All cavalry were armed with sabres, pistols, and a carbine.

Table 2 presents uniform information for the cavalry known to be involved in the 1711 campaign. Once again the uniforms are those that were worn in 1711 or the best details available from an earlier period. As before some details are not known and the entry has been left blank, but once more in cases where it seems possible that the details from an earlier period might still apply, a date is included after the information.

The Russian Artillery

In common with all contemporary armies there was little standardisation in artillery pieces: a wide variety of gun types and calibres were in use. The same was true for battery organisation and equipment. Russian infantry regiments usually had smaller guns, typically three-pounders, attached to them at the usual rate of one gun per battalion. These attached guns were at least partly manned by personnel from the parent regiment, a common practice in the later eighteenth century but an innovation at the time. There would be some gunners with the pieces attached to infantry battalions, and all other guns were wholly manned by artillerymen.

Gunners either wore a black tricorn or a red *karpus* with a blue lining. They were dressed in a red coat with a blue lining and cuffs, red waistcoats, red breeches and blue or blue and white striped stockings. The guns and wagons themselves were painted, but there is disagreement on which colours were used, being either painted red with yellow metalwork or green with black metalwork.

Table 1. Russian Infantry Uniform, 1711

Unit	Hat Lace	Karpus / Cap lining	Coat	Lining / Cuffs	Waistcoat	Breeches	Stockings
Preobrazhenski Guard	Yellow	Green, red	Green	Red	Red (or green)	Red (or green)	Red (or white)
Semenovski Guard	Yellow		Blue	Red	Red (or blue)	Red (or blue)	Red (or white)
Bils' Grenadier		Blue	Blue				
Busch's Grenadier		Blue, red	Blue				
Enzberg's Grenadier			Green		Red		
Repnin's Grenadier		Red, bearskin	Red				
Astrachanski			Green	Red		Leather	
Ingermanlandski	White (1703)		Yellow	Red	Leather	Leather	Red (1706)
Belogorodski		Yellow, red	Blue		Red (1709)	Red or leather (1709)	Red (1709)
Butyrski	Yellow	Yellow, red	Red	White	White	Leather	White
Chernigovski	White?		Green			Green	
Ivangorodski	No lace		Green	Red	Red	Red	Red
Kargopolski	No lace		Green				
Kazanski		Blue, red	Blue	Red			
Kievski	White?		Red	Yellow	Grey	Red	Grey/ yellow stripes
Koporski	White?		Green	Red		Leather	Red
Lefort's		Green, red	Red				
Moskvaski		Red, Yellow (or blue)	Red	Yellow (or blue)	Red (1709)	Red (1709)	Red (1709)
Narvski	No lace		Green	Red		Red or leather	Red
Nizhni Novgorodski	White?	Green, red	Green			Leather	Grey
Novgorodski		White, Green	Green	Red	Red	Red	Red
Pskovski	White?		Green				
Rentzel's		Green, red	Green	Red	Red	Red	Red
Riazinski	No lace		Green				
Rostovski	White?		Green	Yellow		Red	

Unit	Hat Lace	Karpus / Cap lining	Coat	Lining / Cuffs	Waistcoat	Breeches	Stockings
Schlusselburgski		Yellow, red	Green			Leather (1708)	
Sibirski	White?	Green	Green		Red	Red	
Tobolski		Green, red	Green	Red	Red	Red	Red
Tverski		Red	Green	Red	Red	Red	Red
Ustiugski			Light Blue				
Velikoloutski		White, red	White	Blue			
Viatski	White?		Green	Red	Green	Green	Red
Vologdski							
Yamburgski							

Table 2. Russian Cavalry Uniform, 1711

Unit	Hat Lace	Karpus / Cap, lining	Coat	Lining/Cuffs	Waistcoat	Breeches
G. S. Kropotov Horse Grenadier		Green	Green			
Ropp Horse Grenadier	No known details					
Rozhnov Horse Grenadier	No known details					
Azovski	White?		Blue		Leather	Leather
Belozerski	White?		Blue	Red	Red	Red
Leib or Life	Yellow	Red, blue	Blue	Red	Leather	Leather
Kargopolski	White?		Green	Red	Red	Red
Kazanski	No known details					
Moskovski	White?		White	White	Brown	Brown
Nizhni Novgorodski	No known details					
Novgorodski		White, green	Green		Leather	Leather
Permski	White?		White	Red	Red	Red
Pskovski	White?		Blue	Red	Leather	Leather
Ryanzanski	No known details					
St. Peterburgski	White (1707)		Green	Red	Red	Red
Sibirski	White?		Blue	Red	Red	Red
Smolenski		White, red	White	Blue	Leather	Leather
Tverski		Blue, red	Red	Blue		Leather
Vladimirski	No known details					
General's Squadron (Sheremetev's?)	White?		Red	White	Leather	Leather

The Cossacks

The Cossacks were a collection of semi-independent states dominated by the Russians and increasingly wary of this. In the years before the 1711 campaign each of the Cossack groups had been divided over the growing power of Russia over them. Each of the groups had unsuccessfully attempted to revolt or to change sides, and this meant that the Cossacks fought on both sides during the 1711 campaign. The majority fought with the Russians mainly under relatively new, pro-Russian, leadership. Those who sided with the Ottomans were supporters of the former rebel groups or pro-Swedish factions. There were two main troop types in the Cossack army, the light horse that Cossacks were famous for, but also a surprising number of musket-armed infantry.

The light horse specialised in tactics common for this troop type: raiding rear areas, harassing stragglers and skirmishing and so on. They would rarely stand and fight hand-to-hand and charges were only undertaken against demoralised or vulnerable opponents. The infantry specialised in defending fortified positions, either towns and villages or a wagon lager; the dogged defence of fortifications was as much a part of Cossack tactics as light cavalry operations and raids. A proportion of the infantry would also be mounted, it being common for troops to mount or dismount depending on the tactical situation. No details are available for the exact composition of the Cossack forces, but in general a small force was likely to be mainly light horse, only a sizeable force would have a significant proportion of infantry and in this case up to half of the number of a large army could be infantry. Cossacks were divided into regiments and these in turn were divided into varying numbers of *sotnias*, the equivalent of squadrons or companies. *Sotnias* were supposed to comprise 100 men but in practice often varied greatly and could be up to 200 men strong. This in turn meant that the total size of regiments could also vary greatly.

Cossacks did not wear uniforms, and were free to dress as they pleased. They are often depicted wearing kaftans and baggy trousers which are frequently shown tucked into their boots or Turkish-style shoes. On their head they would wear a fur cap or possibly a cloth hat with fur trimming. This maybe seen as 'typical' Cossack clothing but in practice there would be little standardisation, and individual variation. The same is true with weaponry, Cossacks usually carrying a sabre, at least one pistol and a musket which was often the long-barrelled kind found in the East. In addition to this they could add a light lance if fighting mounted, and a variety of other weapons.

The Kalmyks

Very few details on the forces of the Kalmyk Khanate are available. The army largely consisted of horse archers of the type traditional to the steppes, so they would all be armed with a composite bow and a variety of secondary weapons. They wore loose tunics, felt hats and Turkish-style boots, but there was no uniformity and so colours and styles would vary greatly.

It is likely that there were also a smaller number of other troop types on hand, but unfortunately no details are available. It is probable that a small percentage of 'noble cavalry', a few hundred at most, would be present with the army. These would probably have light lances and more personal protection than the other cavalry, maybe even mail coats, together with the usual variety of personal weapons. It is also possible that some infantry were available as the Kalmyk force was a large one, but as the force was also highly mobile these would most likely be mounted musketeers similar to the type called *segban* or *sekban* in the Ottoman army. If any of these previous troop types other than horse archers were present, then they would compose no more than 10 percent of the forces involved.

The Moldavians

The Moldavian army in 1711 consisted of the following troops:

Body Guard: 60 men
Palace Guard: 10 companies of 100 *sekbans* (mounted musketeers)
Four 'German' (i.e. Western European style) infantry regiments of 1,000 men each*
Four Ukrainian Cossack infantry regiments of 1,000 men each*
20 *choragwy* of regular Moldavian light cavalry (Kolorachy)†
Four *choragwy* of Lithuanian Tatar light cavalry†
Two *choragwy* of Beshly Muslim light cavalry†
1,000 provincial feudal levy Kolorachy cavalry
8,000 provincial feudal levy foot
Town Militia (four or five companies per town, 10 in the capital)
Private companies of the nobles – Hinsary (Hussar?)

* The Balkans area provided Arnaut-type musketeers to the Ottoman army. These are similar to the Cossack infantry and you would expect Moldavia to also provide some. Therefore it might be that these regiments are Moldavian and only Cossack in style.
† A *choragwy* is a formation of 30 to 200 men in other armies, and so is likely to be a similar size in this army.

In theory this would produce a considerable force, but real strengths in the field would be considerably lower. Before the campaign the Moldavians pledged to support the Russians with 10,000 men. In his account of the campaign, De Brasey – a French officer in the Russian army – claims the Moldavians, which he calls Walachians, had 15,000 men.[2] Of these he claims 4,000 garrisoned Soroca fortress, 2,000 were in Mogilev and a further 3,000 in the Moldavian capital Lassi. These were to secure Moldavia and the Russians lines of communication. This left around 6,000 Moldavians to join the field army. This seems to be broadly what happened, although the details might not be precise.

During the campaign the Russians were supported by what they called six Moldavian 'regular' regiments and two smaller probably squadron-sized

---

2   J. N. De Brasey, *Mémoires politiques, amusants et satyriques de messire J. N. D. B. C. db L., colonel du régiment de dragons de Casanski et brigadier des armées de S. M. Czarienne*, 1716.

units of cavalry. At the end of the campaign the regiments seemed to have averaged about 830 men each and the squadrons between 60 to 100 men. It therefore seems likely the regiments had a real size of about 1,000 to 1,200 men per regiment and 100 to 120 men per squadron initially. These would have initially numbered 6,000 to 7,000 men.

It seems likely that the units that joined the main Russian army were the cavalry of the army, possibly along with the *sekbans*. The Kolorachy (both regular and feudal), Tatars and Beshly cavalry would have totalled maybe 3,500 to 4,000 men. With the addition of the Hinsary companies and possibly the Body and Palace Guards this could give a mounted group of up to 7,000 men.

The various infantry units do not feature in the active part of the campaign and did not take the field. Instead they would appear to have been used to garrison Moldavia, as noted above. There are no details of how these would have looked exactly or how they were equipped. But it seems likely that the 'German' units were something like standard Western units of the time and the 'Cossacks' like Cossack or Arnaut-type units.

The core of the Moldavian army consisted of light cavalry, and these are called *hussars* by the Russians. It seems likely that Moldavian hussars would therefore wear similar clothing to and have similar equipment to other hussar units of the period. If these were similar to the more famous Hungarian hussars in nature they would be armed with swords, pistols and carbines. The typical outfit of Hungarian hussars at this time was a long coat decorated with embroidery and a fur cap and the Moldavians may have been similar.

After the war many of the members of the Moldavian cavalry regiments entered Russian service as they faced execution if they remained in Ottoman controlled territory. For a time they became regular regiments in the Russian army. These were organised into two and later three regiments under Colonels Kichin, Tanski and Serbin, but were disbanded in 1721 at the end of the Great Northern War.

The Ottomans and their Allies

The Ottomans

The Ottoman forces were divided into two main categories. First there were the *kapu kulu* or household troops, who were permanent troops paid in cash and were the regular elite of the army. The *kapu kulu* troops consisted of elite cavalry units, the artillery, the famous Janissary infantry corps and a number of support corps. The second part of the army was the various kinds of irregular troops who fought under a variety of different arrangements. Some such as the Ottoman heavy cavalry received land grants in return for military service, a system similar to the feudal system. Others were called out for specific purposes or were the troops of local administrators. The bulk of all of the cavalry were heavy cavalry of the above types, which are here collectively called the Sipahi. There were probably smaller groups of other cavalry of various types, including *gonullu* heavy cavalry, *beli* and *deli* light cavalry. Yet these were not numerous and often had specialist roles: for example *deli* were usually used as small units of bodyguards for dignitaries. Similarly the irregular infantry could include small groups of various types.

The bulk of the irregular infantry were musketeers recruited from the native population of the Ottoman-occupied Balkans. These were known by various names but Arnaut, used here, is a generic name used at the time.

Ottoman units were organised into units roughly equivalent to western regiments called *ortas*, but these appear to have varied greatly in size. For example in 1670 the six units of *kapu kulu* cavalry had the following establishments:

Sipahiyan	6,615 men
Ulufeciyan-i yemin	467 men
Gureba-i yemin	355 men
Silahdaran	5,925 men
Ulufeciyan-i yesar	435 men
Gureba-i yesar	273 men

With this kind of variation in numbers amongst the regular units it is probable that the irregular units were also greatly varied in size. The same was true of the troops' clothing as they were drawn from all over the huge geographical area of the Empire's territory. This contained many different national and cultural traditions which would be reflected in the dress of the irregular parts of the army.

The Turkish part of the army often wore long jackets or kaftans, sometimes with lace embroidery, over baggy trousers and Turkish-style boots. High status units such as the *kapu kulu* and Sipahi cavalry could be dressed in rich and expensively decorated materials. The less renowned units would be generally more subdued, however in all cases there would be little uniformity in the colour or style. Some feel of the dress of the army in this era, and its variety, is given by De La Colonie.[3] He wrote:

> There is no uniformity whatever in their clothing. The Janissaries and most of the Turks wear large heavy turbans, long robes, and very wide breeches fastened round the ankle. Others have them very tight on the leg below the knee, a coat half-way down the body, and very scanty turbans indeed. Some have but a jacket only reaching to the belt of the breeches, the sleeves of which are tight fitting and so short that their arms are bare to the elbow; their breeches also stopping short at the knee, their legs and arms bare, and with the little red cap on their heads, these look for all the world like galley slaves. Others, again, are clad in rags and tatters, with a rather scanty mantle only reaching half-way to the ground, which they twist about them according to the weather.

The most famous part of the Ottoman army was the regular infantry corps known as the Janissaries. The Janissaries appear to have worn a uniform, although the exact colours are not always clear. The uniform consisted of a close-fitting tunic with trousers and stockings over which a

---

3   J. C. Horsey (ed.), *The Chronicles of an Old Campaigner, M. De La Colonie 1692–1717* (London: John Murray, 1904), p. 416.

very long kaftan with short sleeves was usually worn. The corners of the kaftan were often pulled up and tucked into the belt. There is contradictory evidence about the precise colour of these various items of dress, perhaps because the various units and sub units wore different colours. However it is clear that uniformity was normal within specific units. On his head the Janissary wore a characteristic white sleeve cap called a *zarcola*, which was usually decorated with a silver or gilt band and frontal plate. It could also be decorated with additional feathers or other embellishments to mark rank and unit distinctions.

Ottoman soldiers could be armed and supplied with a huge variety of weapons and equipment reflecting the diversity of their origins. Some of the troops were equipped with weapons rarely seen on European battlefields. The lower quality infantry being armed with bows, spears, shields and similar out-of-date weapons. These rarely, if ever, featured in front line service in Europe and were not common elsewhere or in other circumstances. In normal circumstances infantry in the field army was now equipped with a firearm of some kind. Most infantry performing garrison or other supporting duties would also be armed with firearms in Europe. By far the two most common types of infantry in the field army were the famous Janissaries and the various types of missile-armed foot, the Arnauts. These infantry were usually armed with muskets, often relatively long barrelled, and possibly with a sidearm, typically a scimitar. Their appearance seems to have varied a lot.

Unfortunately, not much is known about the tactics used by the Ottoman infantry. Darby states that the Janissaries 'would doubtless be the best troops in the world' if they were as disciplined as Germans.[4] Borekci established that the Janissaries used volley firing techniques from an early date, these were similar to those used in the West.[5] At this time this was the kind of firing called countermarching, performed in a deep formation, in which a rank fired and then retired to the rear of the unit to reload while slowly progressing to the front rank again. Uyar and Erickson argue that this tactic was in an earlier era mainly used when in defence and occasionally in attack.[6] It is probably that this, or similar more up-to-date methods of rank firing without countermarching, continued to be used in this period and may have been more commonly in offensive actions. They also mention that Janissaries, amongst others, favoured swift and ferocious attacks with the scimitar in loose formations. Hence the use of fire tactics by the Imperialists, and probably the Russians as well, that maintained a constant fire to discourage these attacks. These cold attacks were usually made when the target had lost coherence, probably after having been preceded by volleys to break the target's coherence.

---

4   J. Darby (printer), *Complete history of the Turks: from their origin, in the year 755, to the year 1718*, 1719, p. 123.

5   G. A. Borekci, 'Contribution to the Military Revolution Debate: The Janissaries Use of Volley Fire During the Long Ottoman–Habsburg War of 1593–1606 and the Problem of Origins', *Acta Orientalia Academiae Scientiarum Hungaricae*, vol. 59 (4), pp. 407–438, 2006.

6   M. Uyar and E. J. Erickson, *A Military History of the Ottomans: From Osman to Atatürk* (Santa Barbara, CA: Praeger Security International, 2009), p. 43.

Ottoman muskets generally seem to have had a greater range than contemporary Western muskets.[7] This is mentioned by various Western sources, such as De La Colonie who campaigned against the Ottomans, in 1717 in his case.[8] It therefore seems likely that the Ottomans used this advantage of range against their opponents. De La Colonie specifically mentions the Arnauts in this context, who are noted as having especially good at long range fire. There is no suggestion that they also charged in a similar manner as the Janissaries so it is possible this was their main tactic. When the Ottomans assaulted the Russian positions on the River Prut the Arnauts are not mentioned as taking part. Infantry would usually be the obvious choice of unit to assault a defended position and the Janissaries were one of the main components of the assault. The other participants in these attacks mentioned are the Sipahi and not the Arnauts. The Sipahi may have attacked dismounted but it is perhaps an indication that the Arnauts did not assault like the Janissaries because the cavalry are mentioned when they are not. The Ottoman infantry might perhaps be in looser formations than their Western opponents but there is no suggestion in the sources that the Ottoman infantry were fighting in particularly dispersed formations.

On balance, then, when on the offensive it seems likely that the infantry relied on long-range firing at first, most likely to cause disorder which could then be exploited. The Janissaries would seek to exploit any disorder caused, or gaps in enemy firing, by charging in with their scimitars. Rank firing could also feature in attack but was more common in defence, when the enemy would close the range and negate the Ottoman range advantage.

As with the infantry, some of the cavalry would also still be carrying such antiquated weapons as lances, bows, and so on. Some of the heavy cavalry would still wear metal helmets and mail shirts, also shields were used. Armour when used was usually worn under the clothing. In general however much of these out-of-date items had been replaced by more modern arms, pistols, carbines and muskets being commonly available to most kinds of soldiers. Older-style armaments were usually restricted to troops from the Asian backwaters of the empire and this contributed to the lower effectiveness of these troops compared to similar troops from other regions. Higher status troops like the Sipahis and regular cavalry may still have carried outmoded arms, but they would more commonly rely on firearms in combat. Similarly the better troops tended to do without armour or have less armour than their less-experienced compatriots.

The cavalry did not fight in ordered formation but were all superb horsemen and very skilled swordsmen.[9] Darby says they were well-mounted but unable to withstand the shock of a Western cavalry attack.[10] They would attack at high speed, accompanied by wild cries, often of *Allah, Allah*, and in loose large groups. If the speed and savagery of the attack created an

---

7   R. Murphey, *Ottoman Warfare 1500–1700* (London: Routledge, 1999), p. 111.

8   Horsey, p. 415.

9   B. Nosworthy, *The Anatomy of Victory: Battle Tactics, 1689–1763* (New York: Hippocrene, 1992), pp. 36–37.

10   Darby, p. 123.

opening the Ottomans would quickly exploit it and cut their enemy to pieces. If not they would use their superb horsemanship to abort the attack and try again, many commentators, for example Ricault,[11] mention they would make three such attempts before moving off. De La Colonie writes in awe of the breakneck speed of the Ottoman attacks, their ability to perform seemingly impossible halts and then fire their muskets before dashing off in a different direction.[12]

The Tatars

The armies of the Crimean Khanate had traditionally been formed mainly of horse archers, and during this era the army still largely consisted of light cavalry using skirmishing tactics. However at this time carbines and pistols were at least as common as bows. Similarly the spears, light lances and shields which were common equipment in earlier times, had by this period become far less widespread. Traditionally early Tatar dress was made of a variety of undyed natural materials, generally furs and different types of wool. This was combined with a range of common Eastern-style clothing such as baggy trousers and Turkish-style boots. With the passage of time and the greater affluence of later periods it was possible that a larger selection of colours and fabrics was in use. This would be particularly true for Tatar social elites who could also still wear mail or other protection. As with all the previous 'tribal' ethnic groups, there would be a great deal of variation of dress in practice.

The Tatar social elite would only form a tiny fraction of any Tatar army, but such a force could contain a variety of other troop types, especially in a large campaign like that of 1711. It is likely that *segban/sekban*-type mounted musketeers would also be available in limited, but greater, numbers than the elite cavalry. The Khanate could also call on other groups who would help protect the homeland. In previous times up to 800 musketeers could be raised from mainly foreign colonists to defend the Crimea. A Tatar militia who were probably armed with mixture of traditional and modern weapons supplemented these. These troops would probably help man the defensive line across the narrowest part of the entrance into the Crimean Peninsular. It is likely that in the 1711 campaign, which included Russian offensive operations against the Crimean heartland, that these troops would be present with the army. The colonist musketeers would most likely be in Western-style civilian clothes but with a mixture of Eastern-style costume, and the militia would be in standard Tatar dress. Usually light cavalry were likely to form the vast majority of the army, although they could dismount if required.

The Walachians

Very little detailed information on the makeup of the Walachian army is available. In general it appears to have been similar in composition to the

---

11 P. Ricault, *The History of the Present State of the Ottoman Empire*, 1686, pp. 349–350.
12 Horsey, p. 419.

Moldavian army, with the exception that it was said to be two or three times the size. In the negotiations before the campaign they promised to supply 20,000 troops to aid the Russians, twice the number promised by the Moldavians. Despite this it seems that the two principalities usually sent the same sized contingents to fight with the Ottomans: as in 1683 for example, when the Italian Imperialist General Marsigli,[13] who observed the siege of Vienna, stated that both principalities provided about 4,000 troops each. It does seem likely that the Walachians were capable of fielding a larger army than the Moldavians, probably twice as large.

No details of the organisation of the army or its composition exist. It is likely that overall it was very similar to the Moldavian army but larger. All of the troop types in the Moldavian army of the time might also have been in the Walachian army. In earlier times the cavalry were organised into *sotnias* or squadrons of 100 men. In most likelihood this practice would have continued into the present period, with the squadrons probably organised into regiments of around 1,000 men.

In earlier times the core of the army was light cavalry of a uniquely Walachian type that had possibly persisted to this time, although change is also possible. If it remained as before the men would have worn a characteristic striped and exceptionally long tunic, lynx fur cap and an equally long overcoat. By 1711 it is likely that at least some elements of this costume would remain in use, but now perhaps mixed with other styles from the area. Previously the Walachian cavalry were equipped with a light lance, sword, and a distinctive type of shield, often supplemented by a bow, various other side arms and a few firearms. By 1711 it is likely that many of the cavalry would have lost their light lances and shields and that all would have been equipped with firearms.

The Swedes

A small number of Swedish soldiers are recorded as being with the Crimean Khanate army and some acted as advisors elsewhere. These were mainly the survivors of the Swedish disaster in 1709 who had escaped into Ottoman territory after Poltava. The exact makeup of these troops is not known, but it is likely that as they were attached to mobile, swiftly moving Tatar horsemen they would be cavalry. This is also more likely because the majority of Swedish troops that were not captured in 1709 were the cavalry who escorted Charles XII away from the battlefield shortly before the army surrendered. The two largest groups of escapees were about 80 men from the Drabants bodyguard squadron and around 300 men from the Sodra Skanska cavalry regiment. In addition approximately 300 to 500 men from a variety of other units also escaped at the time and these may have been joined by more stragglers.

Swedish cavalry were dressed in conventional Western style for the period. The uniform generally consisted of a long coat with cuffs and, unusually for the time, turnbacks. Additionally they wore a waistcoat, breeches and a tricorn hat

---

13   L. F. Marsigli, *L'Etat Militaire de l'Empire Ottoman*, 1732.

or sometimes a *karpus* similar to that worn by the Russians. The two regiments mentioned above had blue coats with the same colour cuffs and turnbacks. Their breeches and waistcoats were left a shade of natural leather, although some of the Sodra Skanska Regiment may have had blue waistcoats.

Some Swedes acted as advisors and were with the frontline allied forces. It is not known if any present, or larger groups, actually participated in any action. Swedish cavalry tactics were to charge at the full gallop in a tight formation.

The Cossacks

As previously stated, Cossacks fought on both sides during the 1711 campaign with the majority allied to the Russians whilst those fighting with the Ottomans were rebels or supporters of the Swedes. A number of both groups had fled into Ottoman territory with the Swedish survivors to escape Russian reprisals. The majority of these were likely to be Zaporozhian Cossacks who were the most hostile to the Russians and whose territory was adjacent to Ottoman lands. They would be identical in appearance and equipment to the Cossack groups who were fighting with the Russians, see above for more details.

The Poles and Lithuanians

A group of Polish and Lithuanian refugees were also present with the Ottoman armies. These were supporters of the former king of Poland and Lithuania who had been a puppet ruler installed by the Swedes. They had fled or had been forced to leave their homeland in 1709 following the Swedish defeat in the Ukraine. Regrettably there are no exact details of the composition of these Polish and Lithuanian exiles allied with the Ottomans during the 1711 campaign. At this time Polish and Lithuanian armies were largely composed of cavalry consisting of a mixture of native troops and Western style units. The westernised troops were generally lower status mercenaries fighting for wages, so it is most likely that the troops fighting with the Ottomans were mounted units of native Polish and Lithuanian cavalry. These national troops were made up of hussars, *pancerni*, and *jazda lekka*.

The hussars were the renowned 'winged' heavy cavalry type rather than the lighter-style horsemen originating in Hungary and the Balkans. They wore a metal helmet and body armour and often sported one or two of the famous 'wings' on their backs, a painted wooden frame edge with numerous decorative feathers. They were armed with heavy lance, sabre, pistols and carbine and their clothing and horse furniture was expensive and often ornately decorated but not usually of a standard pattern or design. While the hussars were the heavy cavalry of the army, the *pancerni* were the medium or multi-purpose cavalry. They could be equipped with helmets, mail coats and shields whilst being armed with traditional weapons such as light lances, bows, and so on. However, the most important weapons during this period were sword, pistol, and carbine, and it is likely that the older-style weapons and equipment were increasingly uncommon amongst all types of Polish and Lithuanian cavalry. The hussars only formed a minor part of Polish cavalry at this time, a maximum of 10 percent and probably less than this, whilst the *pancerni* were the backbone of the army and normally the largest percentage of it. There was also a small group of Lithuanian cavalry called *petyhori* who were similar to *pancerni* in dress and equipment but carried heavy lances like the hussars. The *pancerni* were dual-purpose cavalry. They could use the missile weapons to create disorder in an enemy formation before a charge or charge themselves. In a charge they were in theory to support the main charging cavalry, the hussars and *petyhori*, but were also capable of charging alone. The final type of cavalry was the *jazda lekka*, light horse who performed the customary light cavalry duties of skirmishing, scouting, and so on. These were dressed in traditional Polish style and were lightly equipped with bows or more commonly carbines. They also usually contributed the second biggest contingent in the army but only by a small number.

It is likely that there were only a small number of hussars and *petyhori* with the army, probably less than 500. The majority of the army would be *pancerni* but at least a third would be *jazda lekka* light cavalry. Polish and Lithuanian cavalry were organised into 'banners': squadrons or troops which were 30 to 150 men strong. The banners were then organised into regiments of three or more banners.

4

The Crimean, Ukrainian, and Kuban Fronts

This section will look at the secondary theatres in the war, the Crimean, Ukrainian, and Kuban fronts. In each of these theatres the dominant group in the Ottoman forces was the army of the Crimean Khanate, or the Tatars. On the Russian side the core of their troops were the Cossacks and Kalmyks allied to the Russians. The orders of battle of the various combatants will also be discussed in the next two sections, but unfortunately there is a great deal of uncertainty about many aspects of the army organisations in this part of the world at this time. For many of the combatants it is rare to find a detailed breakdown of the units or troop types involved and it is common to only have a figure for the overall size of the army or contingents listed. Yet even this can be problematic, as often the figures quoted are at the best questionable. Frequently the numbers given fluctuate considerably between different sources, and so a judgement has to be made. For example the total size of the Ottoman army varies between 170,000 and 270,000 men for the final stages of the campaign, and modern expert opinion often raises great doubt about even the lower figure for the army size. Finally the numbers given were often manipulated for partisan reasons; as an example, the Russians altered the numbers involved in the 1708 and 1709 campaigns to their advantage for propaganda purposes.[1] Similarly, in Russian sources on the 1711 campaign the size of the Ottoman army seems to be exaggerated to explain why the war went so badly for Russia. For these reasons there is considerable doubt about the actual size and composition of the forces involved in this conflict, as indeed many other wars of this period.

With the declaration of war in 1711 both sides began extensive preparations for major military operations in the upcoming campaigning season. However the forces of the Crimean Khanate and their allies were eager to start hostilities as quickly as feasibly possible, with a raid. One of the Tatars' primary motivations for war was the prospect of the large amount of loot and slaves that could be expected to be gained from such an operation. As previously

---

1   N. A. Dorrell, *The Dawn of the Tsarist Empire* (Nottingham: Partizan Press, 2009).

mentioned, the more or less annual Tatar attacks on the Russians had been prohibited by the terms of the earlier Treaty of Karlowitz. So from the Tatars' point of view the undertaking of these time-honoured activities was long overdue. Many of the allied troops operating with the Tatars were implacable enemies of the Russians, forcibly driven from their homes because of them. So various parts of the gathering Tatar force shared a common desire to strike quickly at the Russians for diverse reasons. However the planned raid also had serious military objectives beyond booty and revenge: it would hopefully disrupt Russian preparations and postpone the opening of their offensive to later in the year. It was well known that Ottoman armies were relatively slow-moving, and the raid would offer a chance to delay the Russians until the main Ottoman army was ready for them.

Opening Moves: Tatar Raids

The first Tatar raid was organised in early January 1711. A force of no more than 40,000 troops, mainly Tatars but including some dissident Cossacks, set out to raid the area along the River Voronezh. In this area the Russians had shipyards and the aim was destroy these. The raid moved towards the shipyards and captured a number of small Russian positions, but the weather was very bad and progress was slow. The weather forced the raid to be abandoned before it reached the Voronezh, and the group returned home.

This was just a temporary setback, and soon a second, larger and better-organised, series of raids were organised. In late January Devlet Girey II, the Tatar Khan, assembled two large forces on either side of the River Dnieper in the Ukraine. On the left bank he took personal command, seconded by his son Bahti Girey, who was probably in effective command. On the right bank Mehmed Girey, another of the Khan's sons, was in command of the second larger group of forces.

The details of Tatar forces were as follows, according to one source:[2]

Left Bank:
> Khan Devlet Girey II and Bahti Girey
> 30,000 to 40,000 Tatars
> 2,000 to 4,000 Cossacks
> 40 Swedish officers acting as advisors
>
> 32,000 to 44,000 men in total

Right Bank:
> Mehmed Girey
> 30,000 to 40,000 Tatars
> 7,000 to 8,000 Cossacks under Orlik
> 3,000 to 5,000 Poles and Lithuanians under Potocki

---

2   О. Г. Санин (O. G. Sanin), *Крымское ханство в Русско–Турецкая Война 1710–11 года (The Crimean Khanate in the Russian–Turkish War of 1710–11)*, 2000.

700 to 1,000 Swedes
400 Janissaries, probably from the Black Sea garrison

41,000 to 54,000 men

Almost certainly, these numbers were theoretical totals only. The actual size of the forces involved during the fighting on these various fronts are difficult to determine and I will briefly discuss them here. By the time the final troops were mobilised for the Russian offensive the combatants had raised substantial armies according to the figures often quoted. If the numbers given for the armies operating here are correct then the Russians, Cossacks and Kalmyks between them had approximately 60,000 troops (around 25,000 Cossacks, 20,000 Kalmyks and 15,000 Russians – see below), whilst the Tatars and their allies had about 75,000 to 100,000 men. These are considerable armies for this period and they are the sort of numbers that, for example, the Duke of Marlborough commanded in the West at the time. Many modern scholars now question the accuracy of such figures and few would accept them at face value.

On the face of it the figures for the Russian and allied forces seem more realistic than those for the Tatars and their allies. The diverse contingents in the Russian coalition were all relatively small and seem to be along the lines of what could be practically expected. As an example, the Cossacks seem to be capable of supplying 5,000 to 10,000 troops to fight for the Russians on the frequently distant battlefields of the Great Northern War, and therefore supplying 25,000 men for a vital campaign near to home seems reasonable. Similarly the numbers given for the Kalmyks and Russians seem plausible. So while the total of 60,000 men is probably an overstatement, it does seem possible that something like this total could be mobilised. However, as implied, it seems highly unlikely that the same can be said to be true for the numbers specified for Tatars and their allies.

With hindsight modern scholarship casts severe doubt on the 75,000 to 100,000 troops attributed to the Tatars, and similarly the numbers of allied troops are probably also inflated. Issues such as finance, transport, supply etc., would make such figures extremely unlikely. It is also doubtful from a practical point of view that circa 60,000 mainly low-quality Russian and allied troops would be sent to confront a force of this size and quality if it really was as large as this. Military logic dictates that to have a reasonable chance of success you would expect an attacking force to have at least a rough numerical parity with the defenders, and more likely a numerical superiority. Yet if the figures are correct they would actually have been outnumbered by the defenders. It is therefore probable that the numbers given for the Tatars and their allies are overstated. Both recent research and practicality suggest that the Tatars could field about 40,000 troops for active operations. This is roughly half the number stated above and it seems likely that similarly the allied contingents would be the same, that is around 10,000 men in total.

If the above is correct then we can estimate the approximate size of the Tatar and allied forces. We know that the right bank force under

Mehmed Girey was the largest. Davis suggests this was about 30,000 men.[3] Approximately 20,000 Tatars and the bulk of the 10,000 allied troops. This would leave about 20,000 Tatars and a few allied troops for the left bank group. A total of about 50,000 men.

Prior to the war with the Ottomans breaking out, the majority of Russian field troops were campaigning in Finland, the Baltic States and northern Germany. The Russians also seem to have been caught by surprise when the Tatars launched their first raid. This meant the Ukraine and adjacent areas were largely garrisoned by older troop types and second class formations. Unfortunately details of these forces are difficult to find and only general information is available. After the initial raid, to oppose further raids the Russians at first relied on two 'corps' to defend the Ukraine against Tatar aggression.

Russian Defensive 'Corps', January 1711
According to one source these were:[4]

Right Bank:
Generals Volkonsky and Vidman with eight dragoon regiments. These units had been sent to the area in late 1710 as the crisis developed.

Probably they were the Moskovski, Nizhni Novgorodski, Novgorodski, Tverski, Azovski, Permski, Ryanzanski and St. Peterburgski regiments. These eight regiments were in Volkonsky's and Vidman's commands later in the year. Two horse grenadier units were also with these commands at that time, but in January they may have been elsewhere.

Left Bank:
General Shidlovski with 10,934 men
Admiral Apraksin with 5,000 Cossacks based at Voronezh

Alternatively Davies suggests instead that troops involved were as follows:[5]

Right Bank:
General Janus with 10 dragoon regiments.

Probably the commands under Volkonsky and Vidman mentioned above with the two horse grenadier units, the Rozhnov and G. S. Kropotov regiments, which were attached to this group later on.

Left Bank:
Buturlin with the Kalmyks and about 7,000 Cossacks

There were probably some Russians troops from the garrison of Voronezh operating with Apraksin; in addition other garrisons across the region would have been involved in defending the Ukraine. The garrison of White

3   B. Davies, *Empire and Military Revolution in Eastern Europe* (London: Continuum, 2011), p. 111.
4   О. Г. Санин (O. G. Sanin), op. cit.
5   Davies, p. 111.

Church (Bila Tserkov or Bialocerkiev), for example, consisted of 500 men of the Annekov Infantry regiment along with several hundred Cossacks under Colonel Tang. It does not seem likely that either of these units were originally part of the 'Defence Corps', rather they were just garrison forces caught up in the action. Similarly four lower class units the Zhavoronkov, Bludov, Verhovski and Jangrek regiments stationed in Azov are noted as 'operating against the Turks' in 1711 but there are no more details and they may be a similar case.

The Annekov regiment mentioned above is a good example of the kind of unit forming the Defence Corps and the garrisons of the area. The exact identity of this formation is debatable as there were two units in the area who could be called by the name 'Annekov'. Annekov could be the name of the contemporary colonel of the regiment or the commander at the time when the unit was raised. Originally all units were known by the name of colonel of the unit, but by this period the first class units had been given a permanent name, usually the name of a Russian province. Lower class units retained the old name format and both of the possible candidates for this regimental title still did this. One unit was commanded by Grigory Annekov while the other was raised by Nikita Annekov, probably a brother of Grigory, and was associated with him although he probably did not personally command it at this time.

The unit commanded by Grigory Annekov had originally been a *streltsi* regiment and an old pre-reform style unit, but in 1706 it was converted to a Western-style infantry unit, at least on paper. It was a garrison unit with little combat experience. Nikita's unit was raised in 1706 in the Ukraine and was supposedly a regular Western-style infantry unit raised from local people, but in reality it too was a garrison unit and was later downgraded to 'land militia' status. It was never really intended to take the field and would have little experience of serious military action. It is not known which of these was the 'Annekov' unit featured in the sources. These two possible candidates for the 'Annekov' regiment stationed at White Church give an excellent illustration of the calibre of units that would probably make up the Defence Corps and the garrisons of the Ukraine.

The raid on the left bank was to be a relatively short-lived affair. The Tatar forces here were also responsible for safeguarding the Tatar lands. These forces attempted to raid the area around Azov but were blocked and repulsed by the defending Russian forces, possibly including the Zhavoronkov, Bludov, Verhovski and Jangrek regiments mentioned above. The defending forces numbered about 16,000 men plus various garrisons. This meant that the two sides on this bank of the Dnieper were roughly equal in numbers. However at the start of the raid the Tatars and their allies under the Khan enjoyed the benefit of surprise, and exploiting this advantage they swept through the lightly defended border area. A number of small towns and fortresses, together with their garrisons, quickly fell to the invaders including the towns of Wolno, Maliwoloda, Noiviwoloda and the forts at Mercovi and Ternocka. The impetus of the attack carried the raiders to the major fortress of Samara but this was much too strong to attack. Even so the raiders burned 150 to 200 small transport boats that the Russians had collected there. By this time the

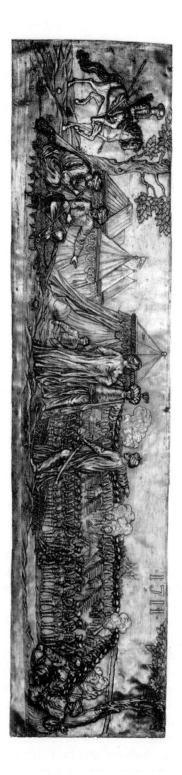

10 & 11. Bas-reliefs

This series of bas-relief plates was created in the early 1720s to be part of the Triumphant Column. Although the project remained unfulfilled, model bas-reliefs represent many campaigns of the Russian troops from 1702 until 1722. The uniforms shown reflect period of production rather than the period depicted. Above (10): The Battle of Pruth, 1711; below (11) and opposite (12): the taking of Derbent, 1722. Images attributed to either Bartolomeo Carlo Rastrelli (1675–1744), or Andrey Nartov (1693–1756).

12. Bas-relief: the taking of Derbent, 1722. Attributed to either Bartolomeo Carlo Rastrelli (1675–1744) or Andrey Nartov (1693–1756).

Tatars had collected a large amount of loot and up to 12,000, mainly civilian, captives who were destined for the slave markets of the East. However by now the Russian and other defenders were alerted and closing in on the raid. In addition the weather also turned and it started to snow heavily. Taking these factors into account and remembering that the raiders were also tasked with the secondary mission of defending Tatar territory, the raiding army turned for home. In late March the Khan arrived back in the Khanate and his part in the raids ended. General Shidlovski and his command followed closely on the heels of the retreating Khan, retaking all of the lost towns and fortresses.

Meanwhile on the right bank of the Dnieper the Tatars and their allies enjoyed a significant numerical advantage, as the defenders in this area could only muster eight regiments under Generals Volkonsky and Vidman. The Russian forces therefore mustered probably no more than 8,000 to 10,000 men. Due to this numerical superiority and the benefit of surprise the men of Mehmed Girey's army had the potential to achieve more than just a raid. Potocki, the commander of the Polish and Lithuanian troops with the Tatars, argued for a move into southern Poland to strike a blow against the Poles who supported the Russians and rally the opposition to the Russians there; at the same time Orlik, the commander of the dissident Cossacks, argued for an attack into the Ukraine with a similar aim. The second option seemed more appealing to Mehmed Girey as the Cossacks would be supporting the Russians directly, as opposed to passive support from the Poles. Therefore the right bank raid headed towards the important Ukrainian city of Kiev. In addition to disrupting Russian plans and possibly taking Kiev, the plan was to gain additional Cossack recruits. Orlik and his followers accompanied this raid with the intention of attracting further support for him and his cause. Because of this the army, in particular the Tatars, were supposed to refrain from their usual practice on raids of taking slaves, looting and pillaging. On 9 March Mehmed issued an appeal to the native Cossacks of the Ukraine to come and join him in overthrowing the Russians who now dominated the Cossack lands. Initially the raid went well and the Tatars managed to restrict their activities. This in turn allowed some more Cossacks to be recruited by Orlik. On 15 March the pro-Russian Cossack leader Skoropadsky was defeated in a clash and further gains by the Tatars and their allies seemed possible.

Mehmed Girey now led his forces into the Ukraine, aiming for the important fortress of White Church, and then Fastov. Once these crucial positions had been secured, the allied forces could hold them and wait for the main Ottoman army to come and join them. This territory would then provide a good base for attacks further north, a strike towards the important city of Kiev. Once again the Tatars moved swiftly and largely unopposed through the border region, capturing many towns and villages. By 25 March the Tatars and their allies had closed on the last obstacle in their path to Kiev, the small garrison of White Church. It seems that the garrison consisted of about 500 men of the Annekov Russian infantry regiment along with several hundred Cossacks under Colonel Tang. Not perhaps the most formidable force to frustrate the advance, but the attacking force consisted largely of cavalry so would take some time to overcome. The forces of Mehmed Girey therefore paused and laid siege to the Russian position. At this point in the raid the unity of the raiders started to falter. Orlik and his Cossacks pressed on with the siege but the other factions within Mehmed Girey's forces were not as dedicated. Each had their own motives, and these surfaced. All of the factions wanted a different outcome for the area if they were successful in capturing it; in short each wanted the area to be under the control of their faction and for it to be used to further their aims. As the siege progressed, the Tatars' restraint started to break down. Over time their patience with the 'no raiding' restraint wore down, and the number of violent attacks grew. The increasing violence towards the local population turned them against the invaders and hardened the resolve of the garrison of White Church.

The turning point of the siege was a sortie by the garrison of White Church and the almost simultaneous arrival of a new Russian force in the area under General Golitsyn, which tipped the balance upon its arrival. Information is sparse about this force's composition but it is likely that it was the advance guard of the main Russian army and probably consisted of first class 'named' units that would subsequently take part in the main attack in the Balkans. This formation appears to have been a fast moving 'flying column', a tactical gambit that was often used by the Russians, where the infantry were probably mounted on horses or riding behind the dragoons, and these infantry could be expected to be of the highest quality as these were generally used in such formations.

General Golitsyn's Force, April 1711

> 9 Russian dragoon regiments
> 2 Russian infantry regiments (each probably with 2 or more battalions)

The failure forced the battered Tatar army to pull back to reorganise and consider its options, and at this moment a Russian flying column of 11,000 men under General Golitsyn arrived and changed the balance of power. The opposing forces were now roughly equal, and the appearance of the Russian flying column was a clear indication that the main Russian army was already on the move and would arrive before the Ottomans. It was obvious therefore that the plan to secure a bridgehead for an attack was no longer viable, and as the forces of Mehmed Girey would be needed intact later in the campaign the Tatars decided to retreat, collecting loot and slaves as they went.

Constant small clashes with the Russians occurred as the army withdrew, and the advancing Russians retook all the positions they had lost earlier. The fortress of Novosergievskaia was retaken on 11 April by the Annenkov infantry regiment, the Akhtyrski, Kharkovski, Tchougouievski, Soumski, Izioumski, Hetman's Cossack regiments and the Voroneski dragoon squadron. On 15 April the Russians claimed they overtook and defeated a large group of raiders, but details regarding this engagement are not clear and by late April the bulk of the Tatars and their allied forces had withdrawn into their own territory and the raid was over. It was now time for the Russians and their allies to strike back.

The Defence of the Crimea and Kuban

With the end of the Tatar raid the second phase of the fighting in these areas began, and the campaign in the Balkans as well. With the Balkans campaign beginning the Tatars needed to send troops to aid their Ottoman allies in their battle against the main Russian army. To counter this, and stop the Tatars sending aid to their allies, the Russians planned for a two-front attack on the Tatar homelands which would force the main body of the Tatar and allied army to defend them. The Russians planned that a force of largely Cossacks and some Russians would attack the Crimean Tatar territory from the Ukraine. This group was under the command of the Cossack Hetman Skoropadsky and Russian general Buturlin, who collected their forces at Perevolochna. This thrust was supported by a second force composed of the Kalmyk army under their Khan Ayuka and contingents of Russians and Cossacks under the Russian commander Apraksin based at Tsaritsyn. This force was intended to join the assault on the Crimea, but as events unfolded they were mainly used to attack the Kuban Tatar territory.

Ukrainian Force at Perevolochna:

Hetman Skoropadsky
20,000 Cossacks (probably made up of mainly Ukrainian Cossacks but with some from other groups)

General Buturlin
7 Russian dragoon regiments
1 Russian infantry regiments

7,178 Russians and 27,178 men in total

Supporting Force at Tsaritsyn:

Admiral Apraksin
This force took part in the initial stage of the Crimean campaign
3 Russian dragoon regiments
3 Russian infantry regiments
6,286 Russians

Kaloshin and Vasilev horse service regiments (old style Russian cavalry)
Suharev *streltsi* Regiment
5,000 Don Cossacks

Khan Ayuka
20,000 Kalmyks

31,286 men in total plus the horse service and *streltsi* units

The identity of the Russian units involved in these forces is not known, but there is some evidence of the involvement of various Russian units in the events of 1711. It isn't possible to be certain if these units did in fact participate and if they did what their roles were or where they were based. Therefore, the following list of units is highly speculative and should be only treated as a list of possible candidates.

Lower Status Units
Eletsky, Ozlovsky and Tambov infantry regiments (detached from the Voronezh garrison)
Lomovsky infantry battalion
Olonets infantry battalion
Voronezhski dragoon squadron

Due in part to the delay caused by the Tatar raids the pro-Russian forces were slow to get going. This meant that the Tatars sent about 40,000 men under Mehmed Girey to Bender to rendezvous with the Ottoman army before the pro-Russian forces made a major move. These 40,000 men were probably those previously led by Mehmed Girey with perhaps 10,000 extra Tatars drawn from the other force, so perhaps 25,000 to 30,000 Tatars and around 10,000 of the other allies. This left a smaller group of Tatar units and allied Cossacks to form the mobile army to defend the Tatar lands. These were under the command of Bahti Girey. It is likely that these would be supplemented by effectively static defence forces manning the fortifications guarding the Crimea peninsula and other locations.

Mobile Forces of Bahti Girey
7,000 to 15,000 Tatars
2,000 to 4,000 Cossacks

Defensive Forces
Probably under Khan Girey's command
5,000 to 10,000 Tatar militia

It was not until late May 1711 that the Russians under General Buturlin and Cossacks under Hetman Skoropadsky started the delayed attack on the Tatar's Crimean heartland. The advance was further delayed by various difficulties on the march and growing interference from the remaining Tatar mobile forces in the area. The main body of the Tatar army was meanwhile marching to join the Ottomans and around 20 June the two forces united on the Danube. Soon after this Skoropadsky and Buturlin learned that the main body of Tatars had already left this area of operation. They had been too slow to achieve their main objective and prevent these troops from leaving the area and joining with the Ottomans. The only option now was to press the attack on the Crimea and hope that if this was successful it would force some or all of the departed Tatar troops to return to this area. This would ease the task facing the Russian Tsar in the Balkans.

The central position of the Tatar defences now focussed on a fortified line across the neck of the Crimean Peninsula. In early June the Russian forces and their allies approached these defences, but they found them to be extremely strong. They had hoped that boats could be used to help with the campaign and bypass at least some of the defences. This plan was foiled by low levels of water not allowing the boats to be used. Seeking a weak point, the main force under Skoropadsky and Buturlin wasted much time scouting the length of the defences and probing for an opportunity to attack. By 2 July Skoropadsky and Buturlin's forces were in position to start attacking the impressive defences of the Crimea. The original intention was that the supporting group based in Azov was to join them in this attack. But the bulk of the Kalmyk forces were delayed and so a relatively small force under Apraksin, most likely the Russian and Cossacks in this group, launched an attack on the Crimea region from the Azov area. The secondary attack was too small to achieve much and was soon repulsed. The larger army led by Skoropadsky and Buturlin also failed to make much of an impact of the formidable Tatar defences. By mid July there was widespread hunger and desertion in Skoropadsky and Buturlin's forces and the growing discouragement of the attacking forces was reinforced by a new Tatar raid. Bahti Girey, leading the available mobile forces, managed to get behind Skoropadsky and Buturlin's army. Soon the Tatar forces were creating havoc behind the pro-Russian forces' lines. By late July the stalemate at the front and the growing desolation in their rear led to increasing despondency amongst Skoropadsky and Buturlin's troops. They had achieved nothing and their situation worsened daily. This together with their apparent failure to prevent the Tatars dispatching reinforcements to the Prut demanded a retreat. On 24 July Skoropadsky and Buturlin's army began to withdraw from the Crimea, having achieved nothing, and not knowing that by this time the main Russian army had already surrendered.

While these events were happening the forces of Admiral Apraksin were camped on the borders of the Kuban awaiting the arrival of the Kalmyk Khan and his 20,000 troops. Apraksin filled his time by probing the defences of the Crimea nearest to his force in an attempt to aid the Crimean attack force. Unbeknownst by all, at this time the war was effectively over as the main Russian army had surrendered, but word of the defeat had yet to arrive in Apraksin's camp. So with the withdrawal of the Crimean attack force and the arrival of the main Kalmyk force, Admiral Apraksin decided that he would strike once more at the Tatars. As the Crimea was so well guarded he decided it best to continue with his planned attack but on the Kuban area, and this proved to be a good decision. With the departure of Mehmed Girey from the area and his brother Bahti leading the raid north into the Ukraine the Kuban area was practically devoid of defending troops. On 17 August the allied forces launched an attack into the Tatar Kuban territories. The combined Kalmyk, Russian,   and Cossack force swept into the Kuban which was only thinly defended. After 15 days the invaders met and defeated the available local Tatar forces, leaving the Kuban wide open. The allied army then proceeded down the River Kuban to the capital of the area, Kopyl, destroying everything in their path. By this time Bahti Girey and the mobile Tatar forces from the Crimea had reacted to events and managed to arrive in the area. The newly arrived force was too small to stop the attack and were soon routed in an engagement but their arrival slowed the progress of the allies. On 6 September news arrived of the events in the Balkans arrived and the pro-Russian allies started to withdraw.

The campaign in the Kuban had been a great Russian success. It was claimed that 38,540 Tatars were killed or captured in the invasion;[6] so were 40,000 horses, 190,000 cattle and 220,000 sheep. Finally 12,107 Russians and Cossacks were freed. Yet the success did not achieve its main objective of keeping the main Tatar force away from the crucial campaign in the Balkans. It came too late to affect the overall campaign which was being played out in the Balkans during the campaign. The main Tatar force had been able to join the Ottoman army on the River Prut and help to win the war.

---

6   Davies, p. 128.

Russian Army: Artillery and Command
Illustration by Maksim Borisov, © Helion & Company Limited
(See colour plate commentaries for full caption)

Russian Army: Cavalry
Illustration by Maksim Borisov, © Helion & Company Limited
(See colour plate commentaries for full caption)

Plate C

Russian Army: Infantry: Command and Grenadiers
Illustration by Maksim Borisov, © Helion & Company Limited
(See colour plate commentaries for full caption)

Russian Army: Infantry
Illustration by Maksim Borisov, © Helion & Company Limited
(See colour plate commentaries for full caption)

Russian Allies: Cossacks
Illustration by Maksim Borisov, © Helion & Company Limited
(See colour plate commentaries for full caption)

Russian Allies: Kalmyks, Moldavians and Walachians
Illustration by Maksim Borisov, © Helion & Company Limited
(See colour plate commentaries for full caption)

Ottoman Allies: Exiled Polish Supporters of Stanisław Leszczyński
and Charles XII of Sweden
Illustration by Maksim Borisov, © Helion & Company Limited
(See colour plate commentaries for full caption)

Ottoman Allies: Tatars and Exiled Swedes
Illustration by Maksim Borisov, © Helion & Company Limited
(See colour plate commentaries for full caption)

Plate I

Ottoman Army: Infantry
Illustration by Maksim Borisov, © Helion & Company Limited
(See colour plate commentaries for full caption)

Ottoman Army: Cavalry

Illustration by Maksim Borisov, © Helion & Company Limited

(See colour plate commentaries for full caption)

Hilt of a broadsword found on Poltava battlefield. Exhibition of Azov Museum. (From the collection of Boris Megorsky)

Plate L

Reenactment group 'Preobrazhensky Life Guard Regiment, 1709'.
(From the collection of Boris Megorsky)

Reenactment group 'Preobrazhensky Life Guard Regiment, 1709'.
(From the collection of Boris Megorsky)

Reenactment group 'Preobrazhensky Life Guard Regiment, 1709'.
(From the collection of Boris Megorsky)

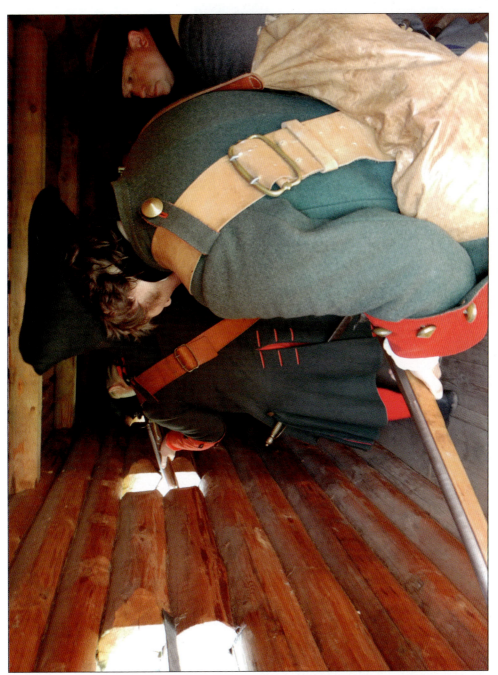

Reenactment group 'Preobrazhensky Life Guard Regiment, 1709'.
(From the collection of Boris Megorsky)

Reenactment group 'Preobrazhensky Life Guard Regiment, 1709'.
(From the collection of Boris Megorsky)

5

The Balkan Front: Orders of Battle and the Opposing Plans

All sides recognised that the Balkan Front would be the principal and most likely the decisive theatre of operations in the campaign. The largest forces on both sides would be deployed in this area, and both sides aimed to secure an advantage with their planned diversions in the other theatres. In the event the Ottoman strategy was largely disrupted by events, although as things would turn out this did not prevent their ultimate success. Victory on this front would bring the humiliation of Tsar Peter and potentially could have radically altered the future shape of Europe.

Opposing Plans

The Ottomans
The Ottoman leadership knew that it would inevitably take time to mass their forces for battle. The timing of the declaration of war and the Tatar raid early in 1711 would give the Ottomans extra time. This, together with the difficulties the Russians would also face moving their forces from northern Europe, would potentially give them the opportunity to strike first.

The plan was for the Ottoman army to assemble in the Edirne/Istanbul area. Once assembled it would to move north to cross the Danube; it was a major obstacle on their route, and had to be crossed to avoid fighting in core Ottoman areas. Once across the Danube the army would continue marching to Bender, this was towards Russian controlled territory. At Bender the Ottoman army expected to be joined by a large part of the Tatar army and other allies, and it was also where the exiled Swedish king was based. Until this time the Tatars were to raid enemy territory and harass any advances they might make. At this time they would be able to join the main Ottoman army and together they would confront the Russians. If possible this would take the form of an invasion of the Ukraine, but this depended on how far the Russians had progressed in their march in the opposite direction. Depending on the speed of the Russian advance, the main confrontation with them could take place somewhere on the route the Russian army was taking, and the Tatars would join the Ottomans in attacking them. This was not excepted to be too far away from Ukrainian territory as the Russians had no base south of this area. It was therefore expected that the Russians would have to proceed slowly from that area, accompanied by a large supply train. The Ottomans also expected to be joined by the Moldavian and Walachian contingents during their march. However the arrival of these contingents and much of the planned Ottoman advance was largely overtaken by events and the Russian plans.

The Russians

The Russians knew that the Ottoman army would be numerous but they aimed to tilt the odds in their favour. They must move fast and they planned to exploit surprise to give them an edge against a dangerous opponent. First of all they had arranged for the mainly Cossack and Kalmyk attacks on the Tatar lands discussed above. The purpose of these were to pin the Tatar forces to the defence of their own lands, or if the Tatars had already departed the area these attacks were to force them to return to defend their homes. This would prevent them adding their valuable strength to the Ottoman army in the Balkans and therefore weaken the opposition the Russians would face directly. In addition they had used diplomacy to further weaken the Ottoman forces and supplement their own. To do this they talked to the Moldavians and Walachians, who were vassal border states of the Ottomans: they were Christian states and hoped that Russian support could bring them independence, or more realistically domination by a more acceptable overlord, the Russians. In the long term these states would greatly enhance Russia's power in the area and perhaps lead to greater freedom for the Christians there. This was later to be a key issue in Russian–Ottoman relations. In the short term it would mean that these two states would withhold their armed forces, use of their fortifications, and access to supplies from the Ottomans, and instead provide these to the Russians.

This could be decisive in the upcoming campaign. With the vassal states' armed forces swapping sides they would provided additional troops to the Russian forces. This was useful, but potentially the most important factor was that it gave the Russians a secure base to confront the Ottomans. The Ottomans had an excellent supply system which had frequently tipped the balance in their favour in previous campaigns; under normal circumstances the Russians would have to rely on a large supply train to operate offensively, and this was usually less efficiently organised than the Ottoman system. The defections would potentially give them the resources and base they would need to achieve success from their newly acquired allies. The defections would surprise the Ottomans and throw their plans into ruin, giving the Russians opportunity to strike deep into Ottoman territory. Therefore, the plan was for the Russian forces to march quickly to Moldavia and Walachia. The Ottomans could then be caught at a disadvantage by the rapidity of the Russian march into the region and the support of the defecting vassal states could be ensured. With the benefit of this position gained by bold action they would achieve a distinct advantage over a badly wrong-footed enemy. The Russians could even get to the Danube before the Ottomans had crossed it. This would cut off the Ottomans from the Russian positions and force the Ottomans to attack across a defended river.

To achieve the required speed of advance the Russians were going to march with a minimum of supplies and rely on their Balkan allies to provide the supplies they needed when they arrived in that area. This was a high risk operation, as the Russians would have to perform a long march over a generally hostile area. A portion of the army under the Russian commander Sheremetev would lead the way and attempt to push forward as fast as possible. The rest of the army would follow on behind, including Tsar Peter himself.

The Ottoman Army

Details of the exact composition of the Ottoman force and even the overall numbers involved are difficult to ascertain. Tsar Peter claimed after the disastrous outcome of the engagement that the Ottoman army had been 220,000 strong, approximately 120,000 cavalry and 100,000 infantry.[1] The Tsar also stated that 50,000 Tatar allies, or 70,000 in some other sources, were also present with the Ottoman army. A total of 270,000 to 290,000 men if correct. There is of course more than a suspicion that these numbers could have been inflated to try to reduce the loss of face suffered by the Tsar and Russians by the defeat on the River Prut. Yet it was common at that time, and since, to ascribe enormous numbers to Ottoman armies. Despite this, these kinds of numbers seem unlikely in the light of modern research. Modern scholars such as Murphey feel that the maximum army the Ottomans were capable of fielding at this time was in the region of 80,000 men for a major campaign such as this.[2] To this figure you could usually add allied contingents from the Tatars, Walachians and Moldavians totalling perhaps 20,000 men. In 1711 the Moldavians would not be with the Ottoman army as they fought with the Russians, but the events of the campaign meant that a much larger Tatar contingent was present than was usually sent. Because of the failed attack on the Tatar homelands the full Tatar army was mobilised and also available for service in this theatre. This could bring the number of allied to perhaps 30,000 to 40,000 men. Therefore modern research would suggest a figure in the order of 100,000 to 120,000 men for the combined Ottoman and allied forces, rather than the 250,000 to 300,000 suggested by older sources.

Other sources perhaps further suggest that the forces facing the Russians were along the lines suggested by modern research. At the time of the Ottoman assaults on the Russian camp there are references to the Russians being outnumber by three to one. In a document from the time of the crisis on the Prut, Tsar Peter says that the army was outnumbered by three to one and because of this, and the situation at the time, he would have to negotiate. This document was written in the field and sent to commanders who were with the army. Therefore, we can perhaps surmise that it reflects accurately the true situation at that time. It would be counterproductive to do

---

1   Peter I, Tsar of Russia, *Journal de Pierre le Grand*, 1774, p. 378.

2   Murphey, pp. 41–43.

otherwise when the recipients of the document could see the true situation for themselves. Other sources such as Bancks' biography also mention the Russians being outnumbered by a factor of three to one.[3] Sutton, the British ambassador to the Ottomans at the time, also mentions that the Ottoman army 'will not be so numerous as they pretend'.[4] According to Sutton, well-informed sources in Constantinople at the time put the army at about 80,000 'fighting men'. Presumably there would also be additional 'non-fighting' men.

Unfortunately this still leaves some areas of doubt, because it is not clear what is meant by the comparison. Peter could be referring only to the Russian forces on the River Prut, which as we will see were about 40,000 men, or alternatively he could be including the Moldavian forces with the main part of Russian army and even the cavalry detachment under Renne. Including these would increase the numbers for the Russian army to perhaps 50,000 men. At the same time the Ottoman forces mentioned may be just the main Ottoman army without the forces under Mehmed Girey or may include all forces. Given the context of the document it seems most likely that it refers to the total available force. Juel, the Danish Minster attached to Peter's court, mentions that the Russian Tsar told him that the Russians had 36,000 men and relatively few cavalry.[5] This is approximately the same size as the army was at the time of the surrender. Juel goes on to say that Peter said he could not fight the Ottomans because they had more than 100,000 men and a lot more cavalry than the Russians. So despite the problems with this reference, it seems to indicate that the Ottoman force confronting Peter's Russians was in the order of 100,000 men and that modern scholarship is generally correct. Although the actual field strength was of course likely to be a lot less than this number.

It therefore seems likely that in reality the Ottoman forces commanded by Grand Vizier Baldaci Mehmed Pasha in the area consisted of 80,000 Ottoman troops and an additional 30,000 to 40,000 allies, as modern research and the situation suggest. It is probable that additional men were with these forces, but in a non-combatant role, as we will see ammunition carriers and craftsmen were listed with the army and perhaps other support forces were also present.

There was also the Walachian army to consider. This army was mobilised and was supposed to be part of the Ottoman forces, yet it is not clear if these are included in any of the figures. For at least the initial part of the campaign this army hung back near the Walachian border awaiting events, and may not have been involved at all. As mentioned above, the size of the Walachian forces is unknown, but seems to have been at least the same size of the Moldavian force and may have been up to three times this size. Therefore the Walachians were probably around 6,000 strong but may have been up to 18,000. It seems likely that the smaller number would represent the number of cavalry that would probably form the field army or the contingent normally sent to the Ottoman army. Perhaps the higher figure is the total forces available, including garrisons for the homeland and lower-quality

---

3   J. Bancks, *The History of the life and reign of the Czar Peter the Great* (London: 1740), p. 161.

4   A. N. Kurat, *The Despatches of Sir Robert Sutton, Ambassador in Constantinople (1710–1714)* (London: The Royal Historical Society, 1953), p. 38.

5   J. Juel, *Ambassade i Rusland, 1709–1711*, 1756.

troops. It is therefore likely that the Walachian field army consisted of about 6,000 cavalry in theory, but probably less in practice. It is more far more difficult to decide whether these troops were included in the lists of Ottoman forces below. Indeed the same is true for the Moldavian forces as both would normally be included in a breakdown of Ottoman forces but did not actually fight with them in this campaign.

The Composition of the Ottoman Forces

The exact composition of the Ottoman forces is difficult to determine, but we do have some information that can perhaps give us the general picture. First of all we will look at several breakdowns of the Ottoman army during this campaign.

The first of these more detailed breakdowns purports to come from the opening stages of conflict.[6] Chandler unfortunately does not give his source for this list. Also he believes that this was just the initial force mobilised, and that more were added by the time the active campaign started. This seems unlikely based on modern research and so this probably is the full force mobilised.

Forces Mobilised 1710
20,400 Sipahi cavalry (possibly the elite *kapu kulu* standing units)
23,000 Janissary infantry
20,000 local infantry
36,500 irregular infantry (probably actually cavalry – provincial Sipahi)
7,000 gunners
10,000 ammunition carriers (*cebeci*)
1,500 craftsmen

106,900 combatants and 118,400 men in total

This list is unusual because of the large number of infantry and relatively small number of cavalry it gives. It is possible that this is because the army was still mobilising in 1710. More likely it seems that there are some mistakes in the list: probably, as noted above, the irregular infantry are actually cavalry. This seems to be confirmed by the following army breakdowns.

There are two detailed breakdowns of the army found in diverse sources. They generally agree with the overall picture but give different numbers.

The first list gives the following breakdown.[7] It is contained in the dispatches of the British ambassador to the Ottoman Empire at the time, and is clearly very similar to the list given above. The overall numbers are the same but it gives more detail of the breakdown of troop types.

Foot and Support: 61,500 men in total
20,000 Janissary infantry
10,000 ammunition carriers (*cebeci*)

---

6   D. Chandler, *The Art of Warfare in the Age of Marlborough* (Staplehurst: Spellmount, 1990), p. 74.
7   Kurat, p. 32.

7,000 gunners (*topci*)
1,500 craftsmen (top *arabagesis*)
3,000 Janissary infantry from Egypt
20,000 Rumelian infantry from Albania and Bosnia

Cavalry: 56,900 men in total
20,000 Sipahis
400 Gedicluh Sipahis
36,500 Pashaws of Rumelia and Asia with Zaims and Timariots

Total: 118,400 men

The second, similar, list is as follows. This comes from the papers of General Sheremetev the senior commander of the Russian army in the war.[8]

Foot and Support: 61,803 men in total
20,000 Janissary infantry
3,403 Janissary infantry from Egypt and Damascus
10,000 ammunition carriers (*cebeci*)
7,000 gunners (*topci*)
1,400 workers (craftsmen)
20,000 Albanian and Bosnian infantry

Cavalry: 57,862 men in total
17,773 Sipahis from the four *kapu kulu* corps
20,170 Pasha's household troops
17,873 Zaims and Timariots
2,046 Serdengectis (volunteers who functioned as an elite assault group of the *kapu kulu*)

Total: 119,665 men

These three lists give a broadly similar and consistent picture of the composition of the army. The figures perhaps represent the full strength of the troops that were intended to be in the army. In common with all armies, the actual strength of the army in the field would be less than this, as discussed below. The following list also broadly agrees with the previous ones, but with some variations.

40,000 Janissary infantry
22,000–24,000 Kapikulu Suvarileri (household cavalry)
7,000 gunners (*topci*)
15,000 ammunition carriers (*cebeci*)
3,000–4,000 top *arabacilar* (wagoners)

---

8   Б.П. Шереметева, *Военно-походный журнал фельдмаршала графа Б.П. Шереметева 1711 и 1712*, 1898, p. 9.

65,000–70,000 Eyalet askerleri (provincial troops – probably mixed infantry and cavalry)

Total: 152,000 to 160,000 men

This list gives higher figures for all the categories except the gunners, and most likely is some kind of version of the notational strength of the units intended to be in the army. As discussed it is likely that the real numbers were considerably less than this and in many cases the approximate percentage of the troop types is consistent. The most notable exceptions are the Janissaries and support troops, the ammunition carriers and wagoners/craftsmen. There are 50–100 percent more of these than in the previous lists and probably reflect the official paper strength of the units. The Janissaries, for example, had a paper strength of 43,562 at this time.[9]

The final, and more detailed, breakdown comes from a diplomat attached to the Swedish king's court and in the area at the time.[10] This breakdown is clearly of the theoretical maximum number of troops and is as follows.

Forces Mobilised June to July 1711

Cavalry
20,000 Sipahi cavalry (probably the elite *kapu kulu* standing units)
20,000 Syleksar cavalry (probably provincial Sipahi cavalry)
12,000 Toprakschi cavalry (probably provincial Sipahi cavalry)
10,000 Bosniak cavalry (probably provincial Sipahi cavalry)

62,000 Turkmen, or Turks, in total

30,000 Arabian standards, 100 companies of 300 men (probably provincial Sipahi cavalry)
100,000 Arabian, Tatar and Circassians (probably light cavalry from all sources)

192,000 men in total

Infantry
40,000 Janissaries
10,000 *schetetzi* (probably ammunition carriers)
8,000 *topschi* (gunners)
20,000 Arnauts
6,000 *miserko* (probably wagoners and/or craftsmen)

84,000 men in total
Artillery

9   G. Agoston, 'Military Transformation in the Ottoman Empire and Russia, 1500–1800', *Kritika* 12, no. 2, 2011, p. 305.
10 E. F. Fabrice, *The Genuine Letters of Baron Fabricius*, 1761, pp. 62–63.

50 mortars
200 field guns
100 large cannon

This list is interesting because it possibly gives further indications of the exact details of the army composition. At first this does not seem to be the case as we need to work out what the list means. It seems likely the 'Turkoman or Turk' cavalry are the *kapu kulu* and European provincial cavalry. Judging from previous lists the Sipahi are most likely to be the standing regular units of cavalry, as indicated above. If this is correct it seems likely that the Syleksar, Toprakschi and Bosniak are Sipahi-type heavy cavalry from different parts of the empire in Europe. The Bosniak cavalry could be Balkan light cavalry, but the light cavalry seem to be listed separately, see below. Similarly, the Arabian standards are likely to be the provincial cavalry from the Arabian and other areas of the empire outside Europe. These are most likely to be the Sipahi-type heavy cavalry from these areas, especially as other 'Arabian' cavalry are noted in the next category and these are probably the light cavalry.

The final category of cavalry is the 'Arabian, Tatar and Circassians' cavalry. The Tatar cavalry of this time were largely light skirmishing cavalry. This with the inclusion of a second kind of 'Arabian' cavalry suggests that these troops were the light skirmishing cavalry of the army. The terms used suggest that these were these types of cavalry from Arabia (probably meaning the non-European part of the empire), the Caucasus area and the Ottoman's Tatar allies. It seems likely that this was intended as an overall category for all such cavalry of this type. It is probable that this included other similar groups to the Tatars and Circassians such as the Moldavians and Walachians. As to whether the Moldavians and Walachians are included in this figure, from the course of the campaign it is clear that many of these troops would be unavailable at periods during the campaign. If the Moldavians and Walachians are included then the defection of the Moldavians, and the Walachians' uncertainty, would reduce this figure. Similarly the numbers of Tatars with the army would vary as events elsewhere proceeded.

For the infantry in the last list we have two entries for which it is not clear what category they fall in, the *schetetzi* and the *miserko*. There is uncertainty as to what role these might perform, suggesting that they may be support troops such as the ammunition carriers and wagoners in the first list. This seems likely for the *schetetzi* as it seems likely to be a corruption of the word *cebeci*. This means that if *miserko* are probably the wagoners or craftsmen noted in other lists. With the artillery there are no numbers given for the lighter guns which would also be present. Available sources give figures of between 444 to 456 guns in total, so it could be that these figures reflect the total number of guns with lighter guns included. This total would include many guns of older and inefficient types, many of which would scarcely be classified as 'artillery' in many armies.

This list therefore seems to give a similar breakdown to the previous one concerning the troops on foot. Also like the previous list the numbers given for the regular troops are greater than the other lists, probably for the same reason. In addition, this list possibly gives an indication of the composition of the cavalry in the army. Clearly, the numbers given here are also some version of the official full strength in theory available. In practice the number of provincial cavalry was always a lot less than this due to problems within the system.

All of these troop lists have problems and reservations must remain about the numbers given in them in the light of modern thoughts concerning the real size of the army. However the numbers may give a good indication of the relative proportions of the various troop types. The lists also suffer from confusion about what the troop types given actually mean. In the first list, for example, we have 'local' and 'irregular' infantry but not what kind of troops these might be. The second list probably helps clarify what the 'local' infantry are, as they are probably Albanian and Bosnian infantry. Similarly the 'irregular' infantry are most likely to be cavalry given what we know about the Ottoman army of the period, and the fact that in the other lists these troops seem to be listed as cavalry. Other reasonable guesses can be made as to the identity of other units listed, and why the numbers assigned to each type vary in the different lists.

So on reflection it would seem likely that the lists give a good indication of the breakdown in the proportions of the various contingents available. Yet based on modern research it is likely that the real fighting strength of the army would actually be less than the numbers given. We can now make an attempt to make sense of all of the above to construct a possible composition of the army.

It seems likely that the nominal full strength of the army was something like this:

'Heavy' Cavalry: approx. 56,000 men
About 20,000 'Kapu kulu' standing units and volunteers (regular Sipahi)
About 21,000 European provincial 'heavy' cavalry (Sipahi)
About 15,000 non-European provincial 'heavy' cavalry (Sipahi)

Infantry: approx. 43,000 men
About 23,000 Janissaries
About 20,000 musket-armed provincial infantry (Arnauts)

Artillery and Support Troops: approx. 18,500 men
About 7,000 artillery personnel
About 10,000 ammunition carriers
About 1,500 craftsmen/wagoners

This gives around 117,500 men in total. The army would actually be around 80,000 strong in reality and this is probably the 'fighting men'. The definition of 'fighting men' is not given. It could be that this means the cavalry and infantry only but not the artillery and support troops, these total about 99,000 men. Arguably, the artillery personnel could also be included and this would bring the total to around 106,000. All of these totals are possible and they are 20,000 to 38,000 higher than the probable field strength. This shortfall is probably accounted for by the infantry and artillery personnel, if applicable, being significantly under the strength given. We saw above that perhaps only about 7,000 Janissaries actually participated in the campaign, around 16,000 less than noted. Sutton mentions that the Bosnian and Albanian infantry will actually be around 8,000 men, approximately 12,000 short of what is noted.[11] The other troops on foot would similarly be half the listed strength or less. It is likely that there is a margin of error in the figures above, also the other categories of troops would probably be understrength to some extent. Yet despite these factors, the shortfalls in the infantry, artillery, and support troops would account for the bulk of the excess personnel in the list, whichever way the calculation is made.

A possible breakdown of the army:

'Heavy' Cavalry: no more than 56,000 men
No more than 20,000 *kapu kulu* standing units and volunteers (regular Sipahi)
No more than 21,000 European provincial 'heavy' cavalry (Sipahi)
No more than 15,000 non-European provincial 'heavy' cavalry (Sipahi)

Infantry: no more than 20,000 men
No more than 10,000 Janissaries
No more than 10,000 musket-armed provincial infantry (Arnauts)

Artillery and Support Troops: no more than 10,000 men
No more than 4,000 artillery personnel
No more than 5,000 ammunition carriers
No more than 800 craftsmen/wagoners

The above discussion leaves the issue of the number of light cavalry that were with the army. The light cavalry are only mentioned in the final list and this further suggests that this category is mainly contingents of allied troops. It is possible that a small number of this category are Ottoman troops but probably the majority are Tatars, Moldavians and Walachians. Judging by the fact that the numbers given for the other non-regular cavalry are about twice those that were actually present, it seems likely that the potential numbers of light cavalry actually present would be the same. Therefore there were probably a maximum of around 50,000 light cavalry, potentially available, mainly allied, to supplement the Ottoman forces. With the known sizes of contingents we can expect around 10,000 of these to be the combined Moldavian and Walachian contingent, with about half from each. The Tatars seem to be capable of fielding 40,000 men and so it is likely that they would provide the bulk of the rest of the light cavalry category. Of course in the event the Moldavians did not join the Ottomans, and the Walachians only reluctantly. The bulk of the Tatar cavalry would also initially be campaigning elsewhere and few of these troops would be with the main Ottoman army

---

11 Kurat, p. 45.

at first. As the campaigned developed, a lot of allied light cavalry arrived to support the Ottoman forces and bring the number of these kinds of troops available to around 40,000. Around 5,000 or 6,000 of these were Walachians and perhaps 25,000 to 30,000 Tatars. The rest of the Tatars remained in the Tatar lands. To balance this perhaps 5,000 or 6,000 allied Cossacks and Poles, who would not be included in the original lists, arrived with the Tatars. Possibly non-allied Ottoman light cavalry included in the provincial cavalry category would account for any unaccounted for shortfall, if any.

The Russian and Moldavian forces

In contrast to many of the other forces involved in the war, we have a great deal of information on the breakdown of the Russian and Moldavian troops that fought in the Balkans, at least those that formed the main field army. For the Moldavians there were also some forces which garrisoned the homeland and for the Russians there were similarly some troops which protect the rear areas for which details are not known. Yet neither of these was actively involved in the Balkan campaign so we can concentrate on the main armies.

The main Russian army which operated in the Balkans consisted of 20 cavalry units and 34 infantry regiments which had 75 battalions.[12] To support these troops the Russians also had 122 guns with the main army when it surrendered, and there were probably 10 to 20 guns attached to the cavalry detached from this force. Therefore in total the army probably had between 122 to 142 artillery pieces.

The cavalry operating in this theatre consisted of three horse grenadier regiments, 16 line dragoon regiments and one dragoon 'squadron', as listed below (note: units in italics were not involved in the main actions of the campaign).

Horse grenadier regiments
G. S. Kropotov	Ropp	Rozhnov

Dragoon regiments
Azovski	Belozerski	*Leib or Life*
Kargopolski	Kazanski	Moskoski
Nizhni Novgorodski	Novgorodski	Permski
Pskovski	Ryanzanski	St. Peterburgski
Sibirski	*Smolenski*	Tverski
Vladimirski		

---

12 <http://rusmilhist.blogspot.co.uk/2012/06/1711_25.html> and <http://rusmilhist.blogspot.co.uk/2012/06/1711.html>

Dragoon squadron
General Sheremetev's squadron

There were 34 infantry regiments in the army. The majority of these had two battalions but some had three or four. Following is a list of the regiments in the army (assumed to have two battalions unless otherwise noted).

Guard regiments
Preobrazhenski (4 bns)	Semenovski (3 bns)

Grenadier regiments
Bils'	Busch's	Enzberg's
Repnin's		

'Elite' regiments
Astrachanski	Ingermanlandski (3 bns)

Line regiments
Belogorodski	Butyrski	Chernigovski
Ivangorodski	*Kargopolski*	Kazanski
Kievski (3 bns)	Koporski	Lefort's
Moskvaski (3 bns)	Narvski (3 bns)	Nizhni Novgorodski
Novgorodski	Pskovski	Rentzel's
Riazinski	Rostovski	Schlusselburgski
Sibirski	Tobolski	Tverski
Ustiugski	Velikoloutski	Viatski
Vologdski	*Yamburgski*	

Artillery train
2 x bronze 12 pdr guns
8 x bronze 8 pdr guns
18 x bronze 3 pdr guns
2 x bronze 40 pdr mortars
12 x bronze 6 pdr mortars
9 x iron 6 pdr mortars
1 x bronze 40 pdr howitzer
1 x bronze 20 pdr howitzer
69 x regimental 3 pdr guns (attached to the infantry)

There were probably also some light regimental type guns with the detached flying column at the time of the surrender and most likely about 10 to 20 pieces judging by the number of guns attached to other similar formations.

Of these units, some were used in supporting roles or were not present when the crisis on the Prut unfolded. The Novgorodski and Vologdski infantry regiments were escorting supplies and fell behind the main body. They were then forced to halt as the area between the two groups filled with swarming Tatar cavalry. The group lacked a cavalry escort and so was forced to await events. The Kargopolski and Yamburgski infantry regiments and the Kargopolski and Smolenski dragoons spent the campaign in the Ukraine until after the events of the Prut. They may have been some of the Russian units involved in the fighting in the Crimea. Their exact role is unclear but they joined the main army shortly after it started to withdraw, so they may simply have been detached during the crisis. Perhaps they were securing the lines of communication or on garrison duty. Finally, the *Leib* or Life dragoon regiment accompanied the army until Jassy but remained there during the crisis on the Prut.

The main army was organised into five infantry commands which remained fairly stable during the main phase of the action. These had 30 regiments with 67 battalions and were as follows:

Golitsyn's Command (12 battalions)

Preobrazhenski	Semenovski
Astrachanski	Ingermanlandski

Repnin's Command (16 battalions)

Repnin's grenadiers	Belogorodski	Butyrski
Kievski	Narvski	Rostovski
Tverski		

Enzberg's Command (12 battalions)

Enzberg's grenadiers	Chernigovski	Riazinski
Ustiugski	Velikoloutski	Viatski

Hallart's Command (13 battalions)

Busch's grenadiers	Kazanski	Moskvaski
Nizhni Novgorodski	Pskovski	Sibirski

Weide's Command (14 battalions)

Bils' grenadiers	Ivangorodski	Lefort's
Koporski	Rentzel's	Schlusselburgski
Tobolski		

During the campaign some of the infantry units were detached from this organisation, typically to act as mounted infantry in a flying column, but generally this organisation was maintained or returned to. In contrast the cavalry organisation varied during the campaign and frequently was seemingly ignored.

Initially, and before all units had arrived, the cavalry were organised into three groups:

Volkonsky's Group

Moskovski	Nizhni Novgorodski	Novgorodski
Tverski	G. S. Kropotov (horse grenadiers)	

Vidman's Group

Azovski	Permski	Ryanzanski
St. Peterburgski	Rozhnov (horse grenadiers)	

Weisbach's Group

Belozerski	Kazanski	Sibirski
Vladimirski	Ropp (horse grenadiers)	

From around 24–26 June the cavalry were reorganised into four groups under Volkonsky, Weisbach, Vidman, and Chirkov after the arrival of some late regiments. These four groups were in turn organised into two commands under Rennes and Janus. The location of the General's squadron is unknown.

Janus' Command:

Volkonsky's Group

Azovski	Novgorodski
St. Peterburgski	G. S. Kropotov (horse grenadiers)

Weisbach's Group

Belozerski	Kazanski	Permski
Ropp (horse grenadiers)		

Rennes' Command:

Vidman's Group

Moskovski	Ryanzanski	Vladimirski
Rozhnov (horse grenadiers)		

Chirkov's Group

Nizhni Novgorodski	Pskovski	Sibirski
Tverski		

At the time of the crisis on the Prut the Russian part of the army therefore consisted of 67 infantry battalions and 16 and a half cavalry regiments. When the army surrendered on the Prut it consisted of 31,554 infantry and 6,692 cavalry.[13] In addition to these forces it is likely that there would be a considerable number of gunners, engineers and supply personnel. Zvegintsov says that this part of the army consisted of 65 infantry battalions with two battalions with Renne's detachment. The same source also states that there were nine and a half cavalry regiments with the army, the rest being with Renne. It seems likely that Zvegintsov has confused the Sibirski infantry regiment with the dragoon regiment of the same name. Therefore the army that surrendered consisted of 67 Russian battalion and eight and a

---

13 В. В. Звегинцов (V. V. Zvegintsov), *Русская Армия. Часть 1-я. 1700–1763гг (The Russian army: Part 1 1700–1763)* (1967).

half Russian cavalry regiments. This gives the infantry battalions an average of about 470 men per battalion. Similarly the cavalry had about 790 men per regiment, half that for the squadron.

As mentioned above, Renne's Column was detached at the time disaster overtook the main army and probably consisted of eight Russian cavalry regiments; Zvegintsov says seven Russian cavalry regiments and two infantry battalions. These troops along with 'a few Moldavians' and Walachians reportedly totalled 5,600 men.[14] This would give these cavalry regiments an average strength at the end of the campaign of 680 to 700 men depending on exactly how many Moldavians and Walachians were present. This seems reasonable, and consistent with the additional attritional losses associated with conducting the kind of operation they were undertaking and the operations around Braila.

This gives the Russian army at the end of the conflict a total of about 32,000 infantry and 12,000 cavalry. In addition, there would perhaps be 1,000 to 2,000 gunners and other support personnel with the army. Therefore, at the time of the surrender there were a total of about 45,000 Russian troops active in the area. This was still a significant army at the time of capitulation and of course, the army would have been considerably larger at the start of the campaign. Before attrition and battlefield losses reduced the number of those fit for action at the end of operations, and including detachments not present for the main period of action, the army would have been considerably stronger. The units appear to about two thirds of their full strength, or perhaps a little less. In addition a further three cavalry regiments and eight infantry battalions were also in the theatre but not with the field army.

In the period between the declaration of war and the start of serious campaigning, great efforts had been made to rebuild the units involved to their full size. Most of them were probably understrength because they had seen extensive active service in 1710 and earlier. Banck states that to bring the army up to strength an extra draft of recruits was made.[15] This resulted in Sheremetev receiving 30,000 men from this new levy early in the campaign. To achieve this aim the Russians had formed a number of 'recruits' regiments from fresh drafts in the various Russian provinces. These received 'on the job' training, in effect, during their journey to join up with the assembling assault force. Once these units reached the main army they were disbanded, and the by now march-hardened and fully trained soldiers were allocated to the various weakened regular regiments. Many of these recruits regiments arrived at the invasion camp in late 1710 and early 1711 and so the units in the army should have been extremely strong at the start of the campaign, indeed it is possible that they may even have been larger than their nominal full strength.

The Frenchman De Brasey, who fought in the campaign as a Russian officer, says that the army numbered 79,800 when it was at the River Dniester.[16] This included 1,500 artillery men with 60 guns of four pounder size or larger, plus two to four smaller guns per regiment. At full strength and with the number of units in the army it is probable that the army may have

14 *Ibid.*
15 Bancks, p. 155.
16 De Brasey, p. 43.

numbered something like this kind of number at the start of the campaign. Unfortunately, other details in De Brasey's account do not inspire confidence in his account and he does not give as source for this information. Yet the figure given, 79,800, is specific enough to suggest a more reliable source than De Brasey lies behind the information. As it also seems an effort was made to provide recruits for the army, and De Brasey's account is generally reasonably accurate, perhaps he gives an accurate idea of the kind of size of the army, i.e. that it was near full strength.

In theory at least the army was under the command of the senior Russian general of the time, Count Boris Sheremetev, however when the Tsar was with the army it is debatable how much real control Sheremetev exercised. Peter had insisted on working his way up through the ranks rather than simply taking command of the army, and at this point in his 'career', the Tsar had reached the position where he was officially in command of one army 'division'. At the start of campaign the Russian infantry had been separated into five groups or divisions and the Tsar commanded of one of these formations, while the other four were under the control of Generals Weide, Repnin, Hallard and Rentzel. It is not known how the cavalry were organised, although as Janus and Renne later led largely cavalry detachments it seems likely that they were the senior cavalry commanders when the war started.

From the start of the campaign the Russians made great use of flying columns or *korvolan*. These were fast-moving formations mostly composed of cavalry but possibly with a small number of infantry attached together with a few light guns. The infantry were sometimes mounted on horses of their own or rode behind a cavalryman. Zvengintsov gives some details of these formations.[17] Early in the campaign General Golitsyn led such a force consisting of nine cavalry and two infantry regiments, and later on General Sheremetev was in command of 12,000 cavalry with two mounted infantry units attached. We have no details of which units were used in these cases, but with two later flying columns we do. General Janus commanded a flying column or advance guard of 14 and a half regiments of cavalry and two regiments of infantry during the opening part of the campaign.

Janus' Column:
Cavalry Contingent
Horse grenadier regiments:

G. S. Kropotov	Ropp	Rozhnov

Dragoon regiments:

Belozerski	Kazanski	Moskovski
Nizhni Novgorodski	Novgorodski	Permski
Ryanzanski	St Peterburgski	Sibirski
Tverski	Vladimirski	

General Sheremetev's dragoon squadron

17　В. В. Звегинцов (V. V. Zvegintsov), op. cit.

Mounted Infantry Contingent
Astrachanski regiment (two battalions)
Ingermanlandski regiment (three battalions)

Artillery
Twelve light guns

As the crisis on the River Prut developed a flying column was dispatched from the main army under General Renne, consisting of the following units according to Zvegintsov:

Renne's Column
Cavalry Contingent
Horse grenadier regiment:
Rozhnov

Dragoon regiments:
Moskovski	Nizhni Novgorodski	Pskovski
Ryanzanski	Tverski	Vladimirski

Mounted Infantry Contingent*
Sibirski regiment (two battalions) *or*
Sibirski dragoon regiment

Artillery
There may have been some light guns with this force but it is unknown how many if there were, around 10 to 12 would be likely.

Moldavians
Two small units (squadrons?) – 'a few hundred'

Walachians
Foma Cantacuzene and his small group of 30 to 50 Walachian followers

* Most likely Zvegintsov has mistakenly assigned the infantry regiment to this group: it is more likely that it was the dragoon regiment.

The Russian main army was to be joined by the Moldavian army under Dimitrie Cantemir although General Neculce actually commanded the troops in the field. Only part of the Moldavian army actually campaigned with the Russians because of the need to garrison vital points. The bulk of the Moldavians, consisting of about 5,000 troops and almost certainly hussars, fought with the main army on the Prut, although in addition 'a few hundred' were with Renne's column on detached duty.

The Moldavians seemed to have had six 'regular' hussar regiments and two smaller units, possibly squadrons with the Russian forces. At Stanilesti there were about 5,000 Moldavian light cavalry, most likely the six regular regiments, and if this is so they numbered about 830 per regiment. The two small units appear to be with Renne at this time and to be 60 to 100 men each. Probably these units were reduced in strength from those available initially; perhaps initially they numbered 6,000 to 7,000 men. After the war the Moldavian units went into exile along with Cantemir and became part of the Russian army as six hussar regiments. At this time they were named after their colonels and called A. Kichich's, V. Tanskov's, M. Brashevjan's and Serbin's regiments with the colonels of the other two regiments being unknown. It seems likely that at least some of these colonels had commanded during the 1711 campaign.

Finally, there are a number of mentions of Cossacks present with the Russian forces in this area. No indications of their numbers or where they had come from are given. It is possible that some Cossacks had attached themselves at some point, but if so they seem to have left no record and presumably must have been a relatively small contingent. In many cases it is possible that the 'Cossacks' are really misidentified Moldavians.

In summary the Russians probably fielded around 80,000 initially in this campaign, and were joined by perhaps 6,000 or 7,000 Moldavians during it. By the end of it, losses and detachments had reduced the field army to about 45,000 Russians and 5,000 Moldavians.

6

The Balkan Front: the Campaign

The Opening Moves

Both armies started to form in the later part of 1710 and early 1711. Both armies, or parts of them, had considerable distances to travel and so would have to start moving as soon as possible. The Ottomans assembled around Istanbul and had contingents coming from their territories in the Middle East, Africa and elsewhere. The bulk of the Russian army was in and around the Baltic area, something like 900 to 1,000 miles away from the area they hoped to campaign in.

While the Ottomans summoned the parts of their army to a rendezvous point, it would be more complicated for the Russians: they would first have to assemble the army in the Baltic area and then march south to the campaign area. An order was issued on 20 December 1710 to assemble 22 infantry regiments at Riga and then start the march south. This was delayed by bad weather and a lack of supplies in the area, so it was not until February 1711 that this group was able to proceed. By this time another two infantry regiments had joined the army and others would join en route; seven regiments from Pomerania joined in April. In March and April the Russian Tsar became ill and this meant further delays as the army waited for him to recover before continuing.

Between 12 and 13 April the Russians held a war council at Slutske and issued an invitation to all the oppressed minorities in the Balkans to rise up, join the Russians and win their freedom from their Ottoman overlords. During this council it was determined that the Russians had to get a presence on the Danube as soon as possible, this was the border between Ottoman territory and Russia's Balkan allies. It was also a major obstacle for any army to cross. If the Russians could get there quickly they could prevent the normally sluggish Ottoman army from crossing the Danube easily and secure a fertile base area for themselves and their Moldavian and Walachian allies to organise for the next stage of the campaign. To achieve this aim General Sheremetev, the senior Russian commander, would take personal charge of a flying column of cavalry and mounted infantry, supported by some slower

Right: Map 2. The Balkans Campaign

Russian forces under Sheremetev and Tsar Peter advance into the area and cross the River Dniester around Soroka. The Russian army assembles at Jassy, the capital of their Moldavian allies. Unaware of the location of Ottoman forces a flying column is dispatched to Braila and the main body continues its advance towards the Danube. Meanwhile the Ottoman army has assembled and moves north to cross the River Danube. Tatar and other allied forces assemble at Bender. The Ottoman and allied forces then move to unite and cross the next obstacle in their advance, the River Prut, at Faltcha. The main opposing armies are now close and clash over a three day crisis in the Stanilesti area, leading to the surrender of the Russian army. After a period of negotiation the Russian army is allowed to march away from the area along the dotted line arrow shown.

moving infantry which would act as the advance guard of the army. He was to forge ahead to secure the vital crossings over the three major rivers in the area: the Dniester, the Prut, and the Danube. The core of the flying column seems to have consisted of General Golitsyn's command which was engaged at this time in beating off the Tatar attack into the Ukraine, with additional units added. Sheremetev was instructed to move as quickly as possible and to head straight for the chief crossing point of the Danube that the Ottomans were likely to use, while the Tsar and the bulk of the Russian army would follow on more slowly.

Immediately after the war council Sheremetev set resolutely about his important task, however it was going to be a lot more difficult than was perhaps realised during the council. Sheremetev's command headed south into the area where Mehmed Girey's raid had just been repulsed, which was already suffering from the deleterious effects of the earlier fighting. To this difficulty was now added some uncomfortably hot weather which continued for the rest of the campaign. Sheremetev's advance quickly attracted the attention of the Tatar and allied forces within the vicinity. In a short time his advance was subject to continuous skirmishing and harassment by the Tatar forces. To make life even more difficult for the Russians the Tatars set fire to the grass to deny them forage for their horses; this was a significant problem for a mounted force travelling lightly with limited supplies. If as it seems likely the core of Sheremetev's column was the former corps of Golitsyn then these troops had previous seen action against Mehmed Girey's Tatars in the Ukraine, which probably left them tired and in need of rest and replenishment. All these various problems meant the advance went a lot more slowly than it was originally expected to.

On 26 May Sheremetev reached the River Dniester at Soroka and his command crossed the river on 30 May. However by this time he was two weeks behind the schedule agreed at the war council in April. This was a worrying situation for the Russians as it meant that the Ottoman army could already be across the Danube and so threatening Moldavia and Walachia. In addition to this concern there were mixed reports from the Balkan principalities themselves. The Moldavians had risen and mobilised their army to attack any Ottomans that they found, however there was a complete absence of any news of action from Walachia, which there should have been by now. This was perturbing, but it would have been a lot worse if the Russians had known that while the Walachians had mobilised they were having second thoughts about which side to support. The Walachian army

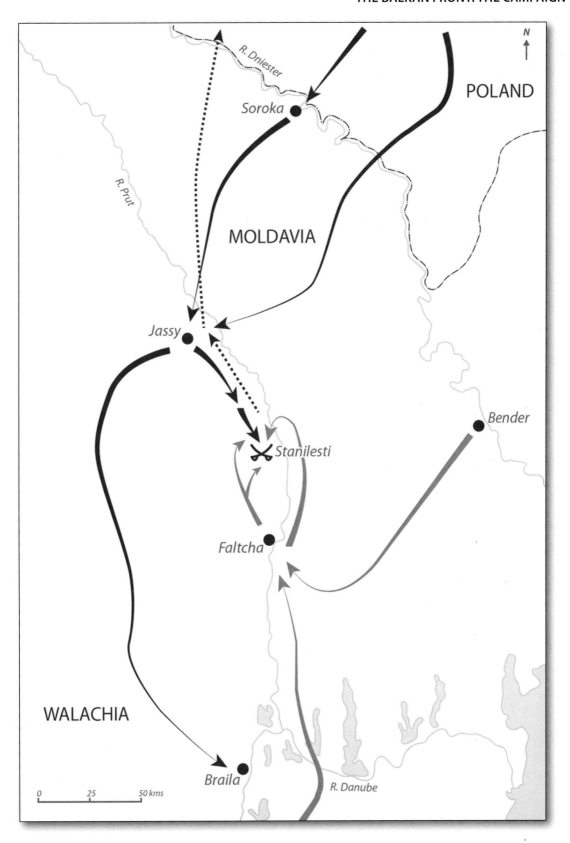

N

POLAND

R. Dniester

Soroka

R. Prut

MOLDAVIA

Jassy

Bender

Stanilesti

Faltcha

WALACHIA

Braila

R. Danube

0   25   50 kms

had assembled and moved to near the Moldavian border, but Constantine Brâncoveanu, the Walachian *hospodar*, was unwilling to take the ultimate step to open rebellion until he was certain that it would succeed. He knew that if the rebellion failed the personal consequences for him would be dire and so the Walachians sat quiescent and awaited the outcome of future events.

Meanwhile, as noted, the Moldavians were in enthusiastic revolt and had attacked any Turks they could find in their midst. Yet it was beginning to dawn on them that the campaign was not going exactly to plan. The expected Russian help had yet to arrive, and when it did it could no longer be supplied. The principality had been plunged into a famine as the result of a plague of locusts and this of course meant that not all the stores that should have been gathered for the advancing Russians were available. All of these factors had caused a great deal of panic in the principality. As soon as Sheremetev arrived at the Dniester on the border of Moldavian territory, he was sent an urgent plea for him to make haste to the Moldavian capital of Jassy instead of to the Danube. The Moldavians argued that they urgently needed support and Sheremetev was inclined to believe them, as he was perhaps convinced that he was already too late and the Ottomans had by now crossed the Danube. If this was the case then a move to secure the Moldavian heartland was essential before it was taken by the Ottomans.

With all this in mind Sheremetev decided that he had to turn aside from his march to the south and go to Jassy instead; he was not to know that in fact the Ottoman army was still not across the Danube. By 5 June his forces had reached the River Prut near to the Moldavian capital, where his presence calmed the Moldavians and they provided him with some much needed supplies. On 12 June his forces, along with the Moldavians, resumed moving cautiously south down the left bank of the Prut towards the Danube. He was still waiting for news from Walachia and information about the whereabouts of the Ottomans. The slow speed of his march was determined by the need to allow the main Russian army to catch up with him, as he was uncertain what opposing forces were now gathering to face him. The Tsar and the main body of the Russian army were now catching up and by 18 June had reached the Dniester at Soroka. The Kargopolski and Yamburgski infantry regiments and the Kargopolski and Smolenski dragoons had by this time been detached from the forces moving south. They spent the remainder of the active campaign in the Ukraine until after the events of the Prut. They may have been some of the Russian units involved in the fighting in the Crimea, but their main purpose was to secure the rear of the Russian advance. The army was divided about the best way to proceed, and so debated the issue at a conference not attended by Sheremetev. Some of the commanders, mainly the foreign-born ones, wanted to take the safe route and stay near the Dniester. This would be better from the point of view of supplies, but left the rebellious Moldavians and potential Walachian rebels unsupported. Therefore, it was decided to push on as quickly as possible to the Danube, regardless of the risk, to aid their allies. This in turn meant Peter was not pleased that Sheremetev had not pushed on further, but it was too late by this time to do anything about it. During the march all of the Russian forces had suffered, and would continue to suffer, from growing losses due to the extremely hot weather they were now experiencing. Despite the heat the only thing left to do now was push on after Sheremetev and the advance guard.

The main body now moved off to join Sheremetev's command and the Moldavians. By 20 June the Russian main body had crossed the Dniester and from 23–28 June it arrived at Jassy. The Russians had secured Moldavia and had the support of the Moldavian army. They had also received a small group of Walachian nobles, including Foma Cantacuzene the second-highest ranking Walachian, who indicated that the Walachians were keen to also join the Russians. Yet nothing had been heard from *Hospodar* Constantine Brâncoveanu of Walachia and there was no sign of his army. Neither was there any sign of the promised stockpile of supplies with which to support the Russian army. It was clear that the area was not capable of supporting an army that size, and that it would have to move somewhere. At Jassy there was another meeting on 28 June to confer with the Moldavian ruler and to decide what to do next. The Russians thought that the Ottomans had not yet crossed the Danube, and so if they moved quickly they still might reach that objective first. Something also needed to be done about Walachia, and to get the Walachians to commit themselves to the Russian cause, which would also give access to any supplies they might have: the supply situation was worsening every day, one not improved by delays in supplies coming behind the Russian advance. The Novgorodski and Vologdski infantry regiments were no longer with the army as they were escorting supplies from the Ukraine and had fallen behind the main body. They would shortly be forced to halt as the area between the two groups filled with swarming Tatar cavalry and the bridge connecting them was destroyed. The group lacked a cavalry escort and so was forced to await events. Once again opinions were split, as dividing the army when the location of the enemy was unknown could be risky. On the morning of the conference perhaps as many as 20,000 Tatars attacked Sheremetev's camp, killing 280 dragoons.[1] This was a worrying event, but it was decided that the army must push on and attempt to complete both objectives.

The plan decided on at the conference was for about half of the remaining Russian cavalry (see Renne's Column, above), to be detached from the army and sent to Walachia: this amounted to eight cavalry regiments. Cantacuzene and the Walachian nobles claimed this would be enough to bring the *hospodar* to declare himself for the Russians at last, and they accompanied this force. It did take the force away from the main army and it would potentially have to deal with hostile forces on the way, including the Ottoman fortress at Braila. One other Russian cavalry regiment, the Life or *Leib* regiment, and the Moldavian infantry, were left at Jassy to secure that place. The other half of the remaining Russian cavalry (eight more regiments and the squadron), the Moldavian cavalry and the main body of the Russian infantry and artillery would march down the left bank of the Prut towards the Danube. The two groups left the Jassy area on 28 June and headed off in two different directions.

---

1   Davies, p. 116.

Meanwhile, unknown to the Russians, the Ottomans had also been active. The main army had left its assembly area near Istanbul in the period 10–14 May. By mid June they had reached the Danube and from 18–20 June they crossed this major obstacle in their path. The Russians did not know it, but they would not be able to stop them crossing the Danube as they planned. The main Ottoman army was now in contact with the Tatar and other allied troops that were to aid them in the upcoming actions. The army was still separated from the Russians as they were on the opposite side, the right bank, of the River Prut and also some distance away. The progress of the Ottoman army's march to the area, and their crossing the Danube before the Russians, was undoubtedly part of the reason for the ambivalence of Brâncoveanu and the Walachians. The Ottomans were within easy striking distance of Walachia, and the Russians were still distant on the other side of the Prut. Brâncoveanu believed he only had one choice, and he reluctantly moved to carry out his military obligation to his Ottoman masters. A few Walachians did join the Russians but the opportunity to gain the support of the bulk of the principality's forces had been lost. It is not clear if the Walachians actually participated in the following events, or if they did participate, how enthusiastically they did so. The Walachian prince could now only hope that the Ottomans did not discover his attempted betrayal, and he attempted to play the loyal subject. Unfortunately this was not to be the case and he was eventually replaced and executed for his treachery.

Over the final days of June and early days of July the Russians pushed south towards the junction of the Prut and the Danube, while continuing to suffer greatly from the hot weather. Here they still hoped they could stop the Ottomans crossing, having not yet heard that they had done so. In contrast, the Ottomans were well informed of Russian progress as they moved up the Prut to intercept the Russian movement. They also planned to cross to the left bank of the Prut to block the Russian advance, at a place called Faltcha.

The major confrontation between the main armies was approaching, but the military balance had shifted since the campaign began. Four infantry regiments, eight battalions, and three dragoon regiments had been detached for various reasons from the main group of Russian forces. These units totalled perhaps 9,000 men at full strength. This loss was partially compensated by the addition of perhaps 7,000 Moldavian troops. In contrast the Ottoman army had received substantial Tatar and other reinforcements, perhaps 40,000 men which was around a 50 percent addition. Both sides would have losses that were normal when campaigning, from sickness, desertion, straggling, and so on. The Ottomans had a highly efficient supply system which aimed to minimise this. Their mobilisation and subsequent movements were slow and deliberate, which would also avoid such problems. Therefore the Ottoman losses would have been minimal and the army would perhaps still number around 80,000 men. In contrast the Russian army had marched a long way at a relatively quick pace, often without adequate supplies and in difficult conditions. It is difficult to judge what the impact of this would have been; losses in the order of 10 percent to 20 percent were common in most armies at this time over a campaign. Given the conditions of the Russian march it seems probable that they would have suffered on this scale, or even greater. This would amount to probably at least 10,000 to 15,000 men and possibly more. In the final days before the main encounter conditions were particularly bad. Hunger and thirst grew daily as the Russians headed south in very hot weather. Sutton mentions that 5,000 or more men had been lost even before the enemy was contacted.[2] The effect of this had probably reduced the Russian main army from around 80,000 men to something like 50,000 to 60,000 men by the time they finally met the main Ottoman army. Of these perhaps 8,000 were with Renne and would miss the upcoming confrontation. The main Ottoman army, in contrast, had grown with the arrival of its allies. and also from being around 80,000 it was probably now something like 100,000 to 120,000 men.

At some point on 4 or 5 July the Russians finally received news that the Ottomans had not only crossed the Danube but even worse that they could be close by. On 5 July Colonel Ropp leading a group of about 1,000 Russian mounted grenadiers – possibly his own regiment but probably foot grenadiers mounted for the occasion – and Moldavian scouts was sent back to investigate what was happening in the army's rear area. This force soon discovered that a large group of Tatars, perhaps 20,000, had destroyed the bridge the Russians had constructed and were following the Russian army. At the same time Janus was sent ahead of the main army with a group of six Russian cavalry regiments, a few hundred Moldavian cavalry and a small number of light guns, Bruce says 12 and Darby 10.[3] Two of these Russian units were 'grenadiers' and were probably the two horse grenadier units remaining with the army or possibly foot grenadiers mounted on horses for the expedition. This group was to ride ahead of the rest of the army to investigate the location where the Russians thought the Ottoman army might attempt to cross the Prut to attack them. They seem to have had orders to capture and hold any bridges they found the Ottomans constructing. If this was not possible, they were to attempt to destroy any bridges found. The rest of the Russian army consisting of the bulk of the Russian infantry and artillery, the remaining Moldavians, and the only two remaining Russian cavalry units still with the army would follow.

The Armies Clash

The Ottomans managed to get ahead of the advancing Russians and on 6 July the Ottomans reached Faltcha where they intended to cross the Prut. On the following day, 7 July, the Ottomans started to cross the river. By this time Janus' force had also arrived in the Faltcha area, they were on high ground overlooking a plain and the river. At around 11:00 a.m. Janus' scouts arrived at a position to look out across the plain to see an unwelcome scene. The plain had a scattering of Ottoman cavalry riding across it, while behind them the Ottomans had already managed to partially bridge the river. They were

---

2   Kurat, p. 65.
3   P. H. Bruce, *Memoirs of Peter Henry Bruce Esq. A Military Officer in the Service of Prussia, Russia and Great Britain*, 1783; J. Darby (printer), *Complete history of the Turks: from their origin, in the year 755, to the year 1718*, 1719.

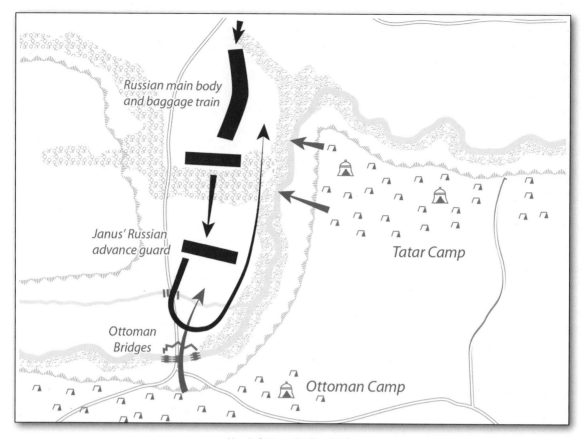

Map 3. Crisis on the Prut: 7 July

The Russian army is moving towards a potential crossing point over the Prut. An advance guard under Janus is sent ahead of the slow moving main body of the army. This advance guard force discovers that the Ottoman army has already established a bridgehead over the river and is building more bridges to support this. The Ottoman, Tatar and allied forces are assembling in the area. Janus advances to try to eliminate the bridgehead but growing Ottoman opposition halts this and soon the Russian advance guard is in danger of being eliminated. The advance guards now retreats back to the main body under growing attack. During the day the main body also comes under increasing attack as opposing forces enter the area.

constructing two bridges and a completed defensive position and palisade protected these. A contingent of Janissaries defended the construction site and troops were crossing the river on the bridges. However, only a limited number of Ottoman troops had managed to traverse the river and crossing could not be achieved quickly, although in some cases the Ottomans had crossed simply by swimming.

Janus had a powerful force of probably around 6,000 troops, and with decisive action it was possible that he could capture or destroy the fledgling Ottoman bridgehead before it could be reinforced. This is indeed what his instructions were to do if possible, yet this is not what he chose to do. Yet Janus seems to have been convinced that he was facing 15,000 or more enemy troops. Therefore Janus made no attempt to attack, and instead he ordered the troops to dismount and form into a single large square. Other reports suggest that there were only around 2,000 Janissaries and 2,000 to 3,000 other troops at this time. Sutton says that the Rumelian horse from Albania and Bosnia were particularly distinguished in the following action and so it is likely that some of them were present.[4] The front face consisted of the grenadiers, and the guns were spread around the square. This formation was soon surrounded and under attack by Ottoman troops. Over the next few hours the Russians slowly retreated perhaps a quarter of a mile as the Ottomans continued to harass them. However many Ottomans had originally been present, it seems likely that more arrived to participate in the attack as time passed and more crossed the river. Despite this, the Russians held out until nightfall and at that time the Ottomans withdrew. Janus had perhaps missed an opportunity but his command was intact, and by this time he had been ordered back to the main body of the army. After the Ottomans withdrew the Russians used the cover of night to move back towards the main army. By dawn of 8 July Janus' command was about half a mile from safety when a large group of up to 15,000 Ottoman and Tatar cavalry caught them and started to attack again. Janus quickly received support from the main body and the attacking troops fell back allowing him to rejoin the main army relatively easily.

At around the same time the Russians learned from a captive that the bulk of the Ottoman army had not yet arrived. According to the captive the cavalry would not arrive until that evening and the infantry and artillery not until 9 July. Therefore, having secured the return of Janus' command, the Russians decided to continue the advance. If their information was correct and they moved quickly it was still possible to seriously contest the Ottoman river crossing. Ahead of them the Ottoman forces were gathering on a hill and that would be the first objective. The army formed into a large wedge for the advance with the guard infantry regiments and Hallart's command in the front. The exposed right flank of the Russian formation was secured by a square. Progress was slow but steady and the army advanced up the hill, clearing it of enemy troops as they went. The Ottomans did not make a stand but instead concentrated on harassing the advance by firing on it. It seems likely that at this stage in the confrontation there were relatively few Ottoman and Tatar troops in the area. Poniatowski, who was in the Ottoman camp at the time, and others, claim that this was the case.[5] As evening approached, the slow Russian advance had not been stopped but the Ottoman and Tatar attacks continued and the advance had achieved little. Tsar Peter therefore called a halt and held another conference to decide what to do.

The Russians were still on relatively low ground and the higher ground seemed to be teeming with Ottomans. If the captive was correct, more Ottoman cavalry could be arriving soon. With around half of the Russian cavalry unavailable with Renne's command this would give the Ottomans a massive cavalry superiority. As progress had been so slow, the exposed position the Russians were in at the time would be very vulnerable to cavalry attack. The rest of the Ottoman army was expected to arrive on the following day but some of it could arrive earlier, and also when it did arrive the army would definitely need a defensive position. To press on to secure the high

---

4   Kurat, p. 65.
5   S. Poniatowski, *Remarks on M. de Voltaire's History of Charles XII, King of Sweden*, 1761, pp. 55–91.

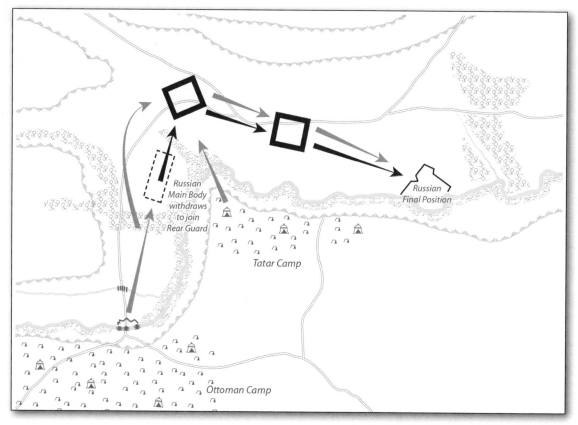

Map 4. Crisis on the Prut: 8 July and the early hours of 9 July

In the face of escalating Ottoman attacks the Russians' main body pulls back. Often in a single large square, the main body moves slowly all day and most of the following night under constant attack from growing Ottoman and allied forces in the area. The Russian rearguard establishes a camp at a place suitable for a st= the army slowly arrives at this position. This camp is on the banks of the River Prut, and frantic efforts are made to fortify the position. The Ottoman army arrives in increasing numbers in the area and launches repeated attacks on the retreating Russians. The Ottomans and their allies follow the beleaguered Russians and set up camps surrounding the Russian position.

ground and attempt to contest the Ottoman crossing of the Prut was therefore too risky. In the circumstances it was thought better to abandon the advance and pull back up to a better defensive position while the number of opposing forces was relatively small. To do this the army would form into a single large square and march away during the night. The cavalry, artillery, and some of the wagons would shelter in the middle of the square. Those wagons or other materials that were not needed were to be burnt or destroyed. Preparations were made for this in the late evening, and when night fell the Russians marched off. The Ottomans saw all of this – including the Russians burning and destroying wagons and materials, a clear sign that they were about to retreat – and came down from the hills to follow them.

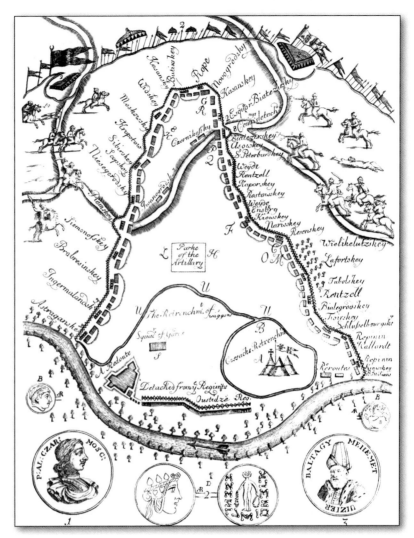

13. The Russian Camp.

This map was drawn by William Hogarth for *de La Motraye's Travels Through Europe, Asia, and Into Parts of Africa* (A. A. De La Motraye, London, 1723). It shows the Russian camp on the Prut River. Across the top are the Ottoman lines and trenches; Ottoman and Tatar cavalry figures are shown attacking the two sides of the camp. These probably represent the harassing attacks that the Tatars, on the right, kept up all day and the Ottomans when a major assault was not occurring. The main defensive line is in the centre and is shown as an inverted 'V' resting on the river. Other depictions generally agree with this, but often have a flatter top. Facing the river are some secondary works guarding the rear of the camp, and also the last ditch retrenchment area. This was bordered by wagons as defences; inside were the civilians and, watched by a guards' detachment, the Russian Tsarina and other dignitaries. It was intended that the army would retreat into this area to make a last stand, if required. The main defensive line is manned by the Russians. On the left, the section next to the river is defended by the elite units of Golitsyn's command. Next to these are the units of Hallart's command with Weide's next in line and covering the top of the V. The cavalry were mainly attached to various parts of the line as individual units, but many few were stationed together in this area. Probably all the Russian cavalry fought dismounted, manning the defences. Coming down the other side of the defences, and mainly facing Tatar attacks, were Enzberg's command and finally Repnin's covering the section on the right where the defences again meet the river.

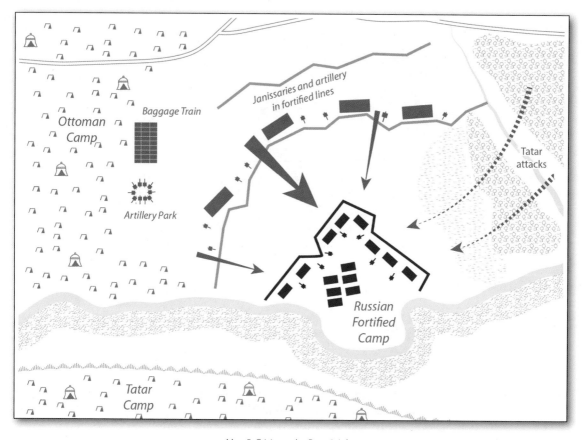

Map 5. Crisis on the Prut: 9 July

With the rear of the army resting on the Prut, the Russian army tries to improve its defences while under harassing attacks. The Ottomans construct their own works to restrict any possible Russian movement while the rest of the army arrives and assaults can be organised. Once the preparations are complete the Ottomans launch full scale assaults on the Russian camp. The main assaults are led by the Janissaries and are concentrated on the vulnerable neck of the Russian position. These attacks are supported by secondary attacks by other Ottoman forces from their newly constructed lines. The Tatars and other allies launch diversionary and harassing attacks on other areas of the Russian camp, but mainly across a marshy area beside it. In prolonged bloody fighting the Russians hang onto their position but their situation is hopeless. Recognising this, the Russians seek terms.

Bruce says that this was a very disorderly retreat with the various parts of the army becoming separated during the night.[6] Often wagons that got into trouble had to be burned to avoid them being left for the Ottomans. He was surprised that the enemy did not seize the chance to exploit the situation, but they were to do so when dawn came. During the night march a large gap opened up between Repnin's command on the right and the rest of the army. At dawn on 9 July the Ottomans spotted it, and seizing the opportunity moved to exploit it. Ottoman and Tatar cavalry, which had been shadowing the Russians, launched attacks and managed to get to some of the wagons exposed by this gap. The Russians halted and beat off the attack but it was to be just the first of many on this day. When possible the Russians continued their progress back towards the Prut, but the repeated Ottoman attacks

---

6   Bruce, p. 50.

made this very slow. This also meant that as the day progressed Ottoman reinforcements arrived, including infantry and artillery. The Russians were already very tired from the previous activities and marching through the night; the day was stiflingly hot, and this with the repeated attacks soon caused them to halt to rest for a few hours, further delaying their move. It was a very tough proposition to maintain any momentum under continuous attack and in stifling hot weather.

Periodically the ferocity of the onslaughts grew to such an extent that the army was forced to halt and they stood on the defensive. Bancks says the troops deployed their portable defences of stakes and *chevaux-de-frise*.[7] From behind these the Russians repulsed repeated and increasingly powerful assaults with disciplined volleys. Bancks also mentions that losses of horses grew as they were vulnerable and easy targets in such attacks. It seems the attacks came mostly from the south on one face of the square, so the Russians were able to rotate their troops around to some extent and get some respite for the exhausted soldiers. By around 5:00 p.m. the first Russian troops arrived at the Prut near to Stanilesti. The river now blocked further movement eastwards and the Ottomans and Tatars quickly moved to block movement in any other direction. The Russians were now very low on provisions and very tired. There was now no choice but to halt and try something else. Here they could stand off the swarming hordes of Ottoman soldiers and they set about building up defences to help them do this. Nevertheless, unless the Ottomans obligingly sacrificed themselves in reckless frontal assaults on the Russians, Russian options were becoming seriously limited.

The Russians took up a roughly upside down V-shaped position beside the Prut near Stanilesti. The river protected the rear, with the flanks resting on the river. On the side of the V facing away from where the main Ottoman army was coming from there was an area of marshy ground. As the Russians settled into this position they set about improving it as much as possible. On the side of the marshy ground this took the form of only the stakes and *chevaux-de-fries*, the *rogatki*. The marshy ground would clearly limit serious attacks from this quarter. Because of this, the other side of the V was concentrated on, along with the area around the point of the V and a smaller part of the other side of the V not covered by the marshy ground. In these more exposed areas an effort was made to build an earth and sand bank to augment the *rogatki*. This was done with some difficultly as the Ottoman attacks continued unabated and indeed grew as more of their army arrived. To build the defences, half of the Russian units built while the other half beat off the Ottoman attacks. Eventually this earth bank reached approximately waist height. The main body of the Ottoman army formed up against the point and the more exposed face of the V. The bulk of the Tatars formed up in and around the marshy area in front of the other face of the V. In addition a large contingent of about 12,000 Tatars, Poles and some Swedes occupied the high ground on the opposite side of the Prut, facing the Russian camp. The Russians were completely surrounded by their enemy. The exposed face of the

---

7   Bancks, p. 329.

V was held by Golitsyn's and Hallart's commands, Golitsyn's next to the river and Hallart's alongside this to the point of the V. The point was obviously vulnerable, and so Weide's command was also in that area mainly in support of Hallart's. Repnin's and Enzberg's commands manned the defences of the side facing the marshy ground, but also with a covering force facing the river. The relatively small number of available Russian cavalry fought dismounted in the front line. Individual units were spread around the perimeter of the defensive line.

The Russian position was strong but not unassailable; the problem was that the Ottomans did not have to attack it if they did not wish to. The position could be improved given time, but time was not on the Russians' side. The Russian army was trapped in a relatively small area with a very limited amount of supplies and in very hot weather. All the Ottomans had to do was wait for the Russians supplies to run out, and the Russians would be forced to surrender with little risk to the Ottomans. The only alternative, if this strategy was followed, would be for the Russians to try to launch a desperate attack, and it was probably better for the Ottomans to strengthen their positions and wait. Poniatowski, the Polish commander attached to the Ottoman high command, says that he and others had tried to convince Grand Vizier Baldaci Mehmed Pasha to follow this strategy but that the Grand Vizier wanted to attack the Russian positions. In contrast Sutton claimed that what followed was the result of action by elements of the Janissaries operating on their own initiative. While this may be true, the attack also involved the Ottoman artillery and heavy cavalry which suggests a more general plan.

Barely had the Russian army settled down and formed their defensive position than the situation took a dramatic turn. For some time the Ottoman infantry, including the famous Janissaries, had been involved in the attacks in small numbers on the Russians during the day. By 7:00 p.m. the Ottoman infantry had filed into position around the exposed sections of the Russian line, and in particular, the Janissaries had taken up station near the vulnerable point of the Russian V. This was a grievous blow for the Russians, as their fortifications were adequate to deal with cavalry attacks but an assault by experienced infantry such as the Janissaries was a different matter. With minimal delay or preparation the Janissaries, with support from the Sipahi cavalry, launched a major assault on the Russian defences. It is probable that the Ottomans were hoping to catch the Russians before they could properly organise themselves or build up their defences. Whether this attack was the result of an order from the Grand Vizier or a local initiative, it did not work as expected.

The Ottomans had been sporadically bombarding the Russian position for some time with the available artillery. At around 7:00 p.m. the Ottomans intensified their artillery bombardment and the attacking troops moved forward. The main assault was to be made by the Janissaries. They were concentrated against a section of the Russian line held by Hallart's command, approximately the middle of the section held by this command. If the Janissaries could break in here they could cut off the greatest concentration of Russians stationed in the point of the V. They would also be able to break into the artillery and baggage train that was in the centre of the Russian position. On either side of this attack were supporting Sipahi cavalry. These deployed in an arc facing the other parts of the vulnerable Russian front line from the river to the marshy ground. It is possible that some or all of the attacking cavalry dismounted for this attack. The Russian position would be very difficult for mounted cavalry to attack. But it is also possible that these attacks were intended to just pin the defenders down and prevent them from sending aid to the sector attacked by the Janissaries. The Ottoman tactics of riding up to troops, firing and then riding off would be effective at doing this, but so too would be dismounting and firing on foot. Whichever was the case, the cavalry did not press their attack, whereas in contrast the attack by the Janissaries was a full blown assault.

Poniatowski tells us that all the Ottoman forces involved in the attack moved into musket range of the Russians, and then most paused to organise themselves for the coming attacks.[8] The exception to this was the Janissaries, who did not stop to organise for the attack but instead carried on straight into it. This perhaps is the origin of Sutton's claim that the attack was the result of the Janissaries acting on their own initiative. Whatever the case, the Janissaries launched themselves in a furious but disorganised attack on the Russian position. Poniatowski says, 'The Janissaries, full of ardor and good resolution, kept still advancing, without attending to the orders; and, setting up a frightful outcry of *Allah! Allah!* many times repeated, to invoke the assistance of God according to their custom, they fell upon the enemies sabre in hand.'

This assault was stopped by a combination of the Russian defences and a point blank general volley by the defenders. Poniatowski continues from the above account. The Janissaries 'would certainly have forced them in this first and vigorous attack, had it not been for the *chevaux de frise*, which the *Muscovites* had thrown before them. A general discharge at the same time, almost in their faces, not only allayed the ardour of the Janissaries, but put them in confusion, and obliged them to a precipitate retreat.'

As the Janissaries pulled back from the first assault their commanders managed to halt and rally some of them. These then attacked again but not as aggressively, and with the same result: the second assault also fell back, and once again some of the Janissaries were rallied. Poniatowski says that at this point he tried to get the commander of the Janissaries to attack in 'more order'. By this he seems to have meant in the manner of European armies of the time, i.e. slower and firing their muskets rather than just relying on an assault with sabres. This idea was rejected by the Ottoman commanders. They did not want to risk a tactical change in a situation, which might become the reason used to blame them for the failure. Therefore, with dusk close the Janissaries launched a third major assault with similar results to the previous two. These attacks were the centre piece of an action which, along with others, were only halted by the arrival of night. The Russian army had survived a severe test and the repulse of the Janissaries had disheartened the Ottoman army. Yet the Russians had shown no inclination to switch to the

---

8   Poniatowski, p. 62.

14. A member of a Russian guard regiment on watch. Reenactment group 'Preobrazhensky Life Guard Regiment, 1709'. (From the collection of Boris Megorsky)

offensive and remained on the defensive despite the success they enjoyed. Tsar Peter considered attempting an attack, but was concerned that the lack of Russian cavalry would leave a gap the Ottomans could exploit if he did.

Sporadic attacks continued during the night but the Ottomans now switched tactics, perhaps belatedly taking the previous advice. They used the cover of night and the continuing attacks to start to construct their own series of defensive works facing the Russian camp. Some artillery had been available for the previous actions, but during the night the rest started to arrive. The Ottomans constructed their works further forward and moved the guns they already had forward into these. As the rest of the artillery arrived it was placed within the growing Ottoman entrenchments surrounding the Russian camp, By this time the whole circumference of the Russian encampment was ringed by the bulk of the Ottoman and allied army, including the opposite bank of the Prut, as most of the army had now arrived in the area. The construction of Ottoman fortifications across the open face of the Russian position meant that the Russians had no room to manoeuvre. The Russians and their Moldavian allies continued to improve their fortifications over time, to help lessen the effects of the Ottoman artillery, but casualties continued to mount. This improvement was helpful but did not solve the basic problem of being trapped. In contrast, the growing Ottoman entrenchment facing the Russians would make any prospective breakout attempt by the Russians extremely difficult. With the arrival of the massive Ottoman artillery train the Russians would soon be suffering from the effects of a tremendous bombardment by the Ottoman guns.

At dawn on 10 July the Russians were in an appalling situation, totally surrounded by an increasingly powerful ring of enemy forces. They were sheltered behind their own defences but in many sections these were very weak and working on improving them was almost impossible. In order to protect the women accompanying the army, amongst whose number was Peter's wife the Tsarina Catherine, a pit had been excavated in the centre of the Russian position. At the same time provisions, water and ammunition were fast running out and everyone was exhausted. The water shortage was not alleviated by the presence of the river to their rear, because the opposite bank and much of the Russians' own side of the river was alive with enemy cavalry who made acquiring water very hazardous. Over the previous few days the baking heat had been debilitating for the troops, and the weather on 10 July was following a similar pattern. The Ottoman artillery was very varied in quality but numerous and at dawn they started their most concentrated bombardment to date. The Russians, thinking that the heavy barrage presaged another major assault by the Janissaries, stood to arms but no onslaught came. The Ottoman army was shaken by the experiences of the previous day and many of the troops were reluctant to launch another full-blooded assault. The Grand Vizier was also reluctant to attack again, and – lacking military experience – seems to have had no idea what to do next. The day became an intense duel between the two sides' artillery with occasional half-hearted attacks by the Ottomans and their allies.

Nightfall once again ended the action and the Russian position remained intact, despite mounting casualties from enemy action and losses from the deteriorating conditions. So far the Ottomans had concentrated their attacks on one part of the Russian line. This, as Bruce argues, allowed the Russians to rotate the troops manning these sections of the line so that weary men could rest.[9] It also meant that the Russians could concentrate their artillery in this area. If the Ottoman attacks had targeted different areas, much of the relatively immobile Russian artillery would be unavailable and rest would be difficult for the troops. Despite this the situation was bleak for the Russians and their allies; the Tsar and the high command could see no way out. It had become clear that if they remained where they were, they would eventually be defeated by starvation and thirst or attrition from the Ottoman artillery and harassing attacks. On 11 July the beleaguered Russians at Stanilesti were still without word of the progress of Renne's column. So with a mood of reckless despair, the Tsar decided that the army must attack the Ottoman trenches in an attempt to break the siege lines. The wearied Russians rose from their entrenchment to attack the enemy fortifications opposite. Hard fighting continued for some time, but in their weakened condition the Russians were incapable of breaking through the Ottoman lines. Bloodied, but claiming to have inflicted heavy losses on their besiegers, they eventually withdrew to their starting positions. This was dismissed as a mere 'sortie' born of desperation, but it seems more likely that it was a genuine attempt to break out and transform the situation that they faced. Whatever the true reason

---

9   Bruce, pp. 51–52.

it is academic, as the attack totally failed, but it did reveal another potential escape route for the despairing Russians: during the attack some prisoners were taken, and these captives indicated that the Janissary corps had taken heavy casualties during the fighting of the last few days and were reluctant to attack again. The truth of these allegations is difficult to ascertain; it could be true, although it is also likely that the Janissaries' supposed reluctance to attack was because they knew further fighting was not necessary to complete the victory. It did, however, lead the Russians to the possible conclusion that the Ottomans might at least be open to negotiation. Therefore, an envoy was dispatched to the Ottoman camp to see if they would discuss terms.

The decision was made to try to seek terms from the Ottomans while their situation was still relatively strong. It was widely expected that any terms offered would be very severe but the alternatives were equally bad. Therefore, a letter was sent by the Russians asking for terms. This move proved to be decisive to the outcome of the campaign and also avoided a potentially dangerous situation for the Russians that was developing at the time. Poniatowski and some of the Ottoman commanders had noticed that the Russian position was weaker in other areas than those that had been attacked over the previous days: notably, the defences facing the marshy ground were considerably less substantial than those attacked up until this time, while the defenders in this area had been thinned in favour of the sectors being attacked as losses mounted. The defenders in this area were also clearly less able to resist because this was the area that units went to when resting. An attack in this area, perhaps combined with lesser attacks in other areas offered the Ottomans a chance for a decisive breakthrough. Some preparations were made to launch these attacks but the Grand Vizier intervened. Baldaci Mehmed had shown that he was no soldier, but he was an experienced politician and negotiator. He therefore cancelled the attack plans and ordered a ceasefire while he discussed a treaty to end the war. The active part of the campaign had finished in this area, but Renne's flying column was still active and the terms of the peace treaty still had to be determined.

7

The Peace, Action at Braila, and the Aftermath

The Tsar and his entourage must have been very apprehensive about the severity of the terms and conditions the Ottomans would impose when they asked to negiotiate. Indeed, amongst the Russian commanders there was some doubt as to whether the Ottomans would negotiate at all, considering the appalling position the Russians found themselves in. So there was some surprise when the Tsar's offer of talks was accepted, but the situation was more complicated than the Russians realised, and the Ottomans had various reasons to agree to negotiations. There was discontent within the Ottoman camp as casualties in the assaults had been heavy; the repulse of the Janissaries in particular had disheartened both them and the rest of the army. Some of the Janissaries even seem to have refused to attack the Russian position again. By this time the Ottomans did not need to attack again, but the discontent within the ranks of the army called into doubt its ability to resist any attempted Russian breakout. The Grand Vizier was not a soldier, and not particularly committed to prosecuting the war to its final conclusion or destroying Russian power. With hindsight, it seems an error not to take this opportunity to set back or stop Russia's rise to Great Power status. Yet Russia was not a very important power in the period before this, and while it had grown in status it was still not clear that this would be a permanent situation. Also there was no particular incentive for the Ottomans to aid its recent Swedish, Polish and Cossack allies who had previously been or potentially could be a great threat to them. As head of the Ottoman government the Grand Vizier also had to worry about getting a good deal for his nation, and other issues such as the possibility of Austrian intervention. Given the nature of politics within the Ottoman Empire he also had to worry about what his enemies were plotting or doing at court while he was away campaigning. There were also rumours that large amounts of gold and other valuables were given to the Grand Vizier and other important officials to induce a favourable attitude. Catherine, who would officially marry Peter the Tsar in 1712 and may have already been married to him in secret, was with the Russian army along with many ladies of the court. It was suggested that Catherine organised a collection of the ladies' jewels to be used for bribery. Given the nature of such transactions there is little concrete evidence that Russian bribery helped convince the Ottoman high command, but as corruption was rife at this time it would not be unusual if it did. Finally, as we will see, events at Braila also meant that the situation was not as favourable to the Ottomans as it might have appeared. It seems likely that the Russians had not received word of the events there, but they must have been a cause for concern for the Ottomans. They knew that their supply lines were under threat from Renne's column. For all these reasons the Ottomans indicated that they were willing to negotiate and so the two antagonists settled down to discuss terms.

Meanwhile Renne's column had been making progress. In late June he had been sent to make contact with the Walachians. His column consisted of eight Russian cavalry regiments, a few hundred Moldavians and Foma Cantacuzene and his small group of Walachian followers, perhaps 8,000 to 9,000 men in total. At this desperate time for the main Russian army, and unbeknownst to them, Renne's flying column was closing in on Braila, on the left bank of the Danube in Walachia. As a vital crossing point for the Ottoman supply lines across the Danube, it was occupied and administered directly by the Ottomans, and had a garrison of around 3,000 men under Daud Pasha. If the main Russian army had known about this they might have attempted to hold out and see if this imminent threat to the Ottoman supply lines would force them to withdraw. The Ottomans of course knew of this force's existence, and were concerned about the effect its mission would have on their operations. If the Russians seized this important position it would cause them supply problems and would open up the possibility of the Russians cooperating with the Walachians. The Russians could also seize supplies in the area and raid more generally to ease the supply problems their army had been suffering from. The Ottomans were worried that their forces in the vicinity of Braila were not strong enough to halt Renne's column, and it was harassed all along its journey. Yet although Renne was assailed by Ottoman detachments all the way to the fortress, he only encountered serious opposition when he finally approached the town of Braila itself. The Ottomans had been taken by surprise by his advance and they had few troops in the area. During the night of 12 July the garrison of Braila attacked Renne's column but with little success. The following day Renne led an assault and captured the town itself, but the surviving defenders managed to retreat into the citadel. However, after a day of preparation, Renne's troops successfully reduced the citadel and the Russians gained full control of the entire town and thus the vital crossing point on 14 July. The fall of Braila had the potential to be the decisive action of the campaign, but it had occurred too late and word of it would not reach the River Prut for some time. The Ottomans successfully intercepted all news from Renne's column, which left the main army little choice.

If the Russian main army had known about Renne's progress they might have tried to hang on. In the absence of this information, and given the plight of the army, the Tsar authorised that practically any terms would be acceptable. Ammunition and food were in short supply and it was expected that the Ottomans would take a very uncompromising attitude. The Russians feared that they would demand sweeping concessions connected with the ongoing war with Sweden and the rule of Russia, and the Tsar instructed the negotiators to offer to return the territory the Russians had taken from them in the earlier Ottoman war. In addition, Peter was prepared to recognise the Polish rebels' candidate for Polish king, return territory taken from the Swedes and even some Russian territory. In short almost anything could be conceded to escape from the predicament the Russians were in. However, once talks started it quickly became clear that the Ottomans were not going to make the kind of demands that the Russians feared and in fact were feeling quite generous given the circumstances.

The Ottomans' allies were amazed at the turn of events and could not believe that they wanted to negotiate at all, considering their advantage. Poniatowski tried to get them to abandon the negotiations, and other representatives of the pro-war parties, the Tatars, Swedes, Poles and Cossacks, also lobbied for this. When it became clear this was not going to work they tried to have harsher terms imposed, and also to have clauses they wished for to be included in the treaty. Over the next few days the negotiations and lobbying continued, but only minor concessions were made to the interests of the various groups opposed to the treaty. The key points of the treaty being discussed called for the Russians to return the territory they had gained in the previous war, notably the vital fortress of Azov and surrounding area. The Russians were to destroy the Black Sea fleet they were constructing and the Taganrog and Kamennyi Zaton forts built around its anchorage. These were key demands of the Ottomans themselves and proved to be their main interest. Other clauses were added in the hope of satisfying the Ottomans' allies. The Russians were to evacuate Poland, where they were campaigning against the Swedes and their allies, and the Swedish king was to be given free passage across the territory dividing him from Sweden. This was clearly something both sides wanted to happen, as by this point both sides wanted Charles XII to leave the area. The Tsar was to conclude peace with the Swedes, although this last stipulation was extremely vague and not effectively enforceable. The Russians were to stop interfering in the affairs of Poland, Moldavia, Walachia and the Cossacks. Finally, the Russians were also to start paying the Crimean Tatar the annual tribute payment that they had paid before the previous war. These amounted to merely minor concessions to the Ottomans' allies to attempt to keep them happy, but they failed to do this.

The main point of contention was the Ottoman demand for Cantemir, the Moldavian leader, to be handed over to them. The Russian negotiator claimed that this could not be done because Cantemir had already fled, which was not true. The other stumbling block in the discussions was the fate of the artillery in the Russian army. The Ottomans wanted the Russians to hand this over, but the Russians claimed they needed it to defend themselves from the Swedes. These problems prolonged the talks for a few days but the Ottomans were not inclined to insist on these conditions. Therefore a treaty was agreed, drawn up and signed on 12 July. Poniatowski, Devlet Girey and Charles XII of Sweden were livid, but the Russians had managed to find a way out of the potentially catastrophic situation in which they found themselves. As soon as possible they departed north fearing an Ottoman change of heart, and scarcely believing their luck. The Ottomans even provided them with supplies.

The end of the fighting did not end the crisis, and it continued to rumble on for many years after the events described. The greatest stumbling block to reconciliation was the Russian reluctance to actually carry out the terms of the treaty agreed on the Prut. Also as Charles XII of Sweden remained in Ottoman territory he was still a cause of friction. Following the evacuation of the combat zone by the Russians and their allies the bulk of the Russian forces immediately marched to northern Europe to continue the war with the Swedes in violation of their agreement. Once the Tsar had escaped from the clutches of the Ottomans he had second thoughts about losing the vital fortress of Azov and the growing Russian fleet being built nearby: the Russians prevaricated in the handover of the city and its surrounding district and similarly delayed the destruction of the new Russian naval vessels in its port at Taganrog. They hoped to delay compliance long enough to successfully conclude their ongoing conflict with the Swedes and enable them time to prepare for another military campaign against the Ottomans to reverse the outcome of 1711.

It did not take long for the Ottomans to suspect Russian duplicity, and over the following few months they constantly pressurised them for full compliance with the Prut treaty, with repeated threats to renew the conflict. A fresh declaration of war in April 1712 and mediation by outside powers finally succeeded in cajoling the Russians into hand over Azov and the surrounding region. In December 1712 a third declaration of war was made to try to force the Russians to leave Poland as they had agreed, and once again active conflict was avoided by mediation, but the Russians still did not abandon Poland. The final stage of 'the peace process' was played out in 1713 and 1714 when the Ottomans once again declared war and this time made serious preparations to resume hostilities. The Russians realised that they could no longer delay them, and with a campaign in Finland about to start they finally complied with the terms agreed in 1711. They dismantled the Black Sea's fleet and honoured the rest of the treaty without any further delay or need for the Ottomans to resort to hostilities.

In September 1714 an event occurred that was to have important ramifications for Ottoman and Russian relations at the time and meant that there could perhaps finally be a proper peace between the two adversaries, at least temporarily. Charles XII of Sweden's residence in the Ottoman Empire had long been a divisive issue between the two powers, and the conspiracy and intrigue surrounding his presence had long poisoned the air and driven the antagonism between them. It was doubtful that 'normal' relations between Russia and the Ottomans could be achieved while Charles remained on Ottoman territory. In 1709 he had been welcome as an honoured guest by the Sultan but the conflict with Russia and other issues had steadily lost the Swedish king friends within the empire, and by 1714 the Ottomans were keen to be rid of this troublesome irritant. He had arrived on Ottoman territory suffering from a serious battle wound. This took time to heal but also became a convenient excuse for the Swedish king to stay and attempt to meddle in Ottoman affairs to further his cause. Yet by 1714 he was long healed and for some time his efforts had achieved little. Charles calculated that he had achieved all that was possible to achieve in the Empire, and it was time to leave. On 20 September he finally left Ottoman territory and effectively ended the crisis that had been caused by his arrival five years before.

Looking back on events of the time many people have seen the lenient terms imposed on the Russians by the Ottomans in 1711 as a decisive moment in relations between the two powers. The Tsar and the best part of his previously victorious army were at the Ottomans' mercy, and if they had taken full advantage of the situation they could have permanently altered the balance of power in their favour. They could also have stopped, or at least postponed, Russia's rise as a Great Power for a significant period of time. However this was not necessarily so apparent at the time and is more discernible with the benefit of hindsight. It is easy to forget that the Ottoman Empire was still a major power during this period; it was after all only a few years earlier that they had besieged the City of Vienna, the gateway to Europe, and they saw no circumstances that would prevent their future prosperity. Neither was it obvious at this time that Russia would be continue to be a major power in the future. Until a short time before these events, Russia had been a minor power that the Ottomans usually left the Tatars to deal with.

The campaign of 1711 showed that the Ottoman army was still a force to be reckoned with as they defeated a victorious and experienced Russian army, many of whom had been present at the momentous Russian victory of Poltava in 1709. It must be kept in mind that the figures given for the forces available to the protagonists are not reliable; the two sides were probably quite closely matched. Taking all the forces involved across all the fronts, the two sides were broadly equal in strength with perhaps a slight Russian advantage, but not a vast one. The Russians and their allies probably fielded about 140,000 men across all fronts, while the Turks and their allies probably numbered 130,000 men again across all fronts. The Turks and their allies succeeded in deflecting Russian operations on the secondary fronts which enabled them to concentrate superior numbers in the decisive theatre of operations. By judicious manoeuvring and better management of logistics they therefore secured perhaps a two to one advantage in troops against the total force of the Russians and their allies in the Balkans. In addition to this numerical advantage must be added the superiority of their supply system. Ottoman armies were renowned for moving slowly not through indolence but because they took great care to ensure adequate provision of supplies at all times. In contrast the Russians' supply arrangements were totally inefficient and in combination with the constant sniping of the Ottoman skirmishers created an exorbitant rate of attrition. Finally they suffered from overconfidence and dividing their forces, in particular the vital cavalry. These detachments and casualties probably increased the Ottomans numerical advantage to three to one at the vital point of the campaign, because the Russian army dwindled away through avoidable losses. They pushed on when the situation ahead was unknown and it was perhaps better to consolidate, while the lack of cavalry remaining with the main army severely limited their operations.

The Ottoman victory in 1711 was a great achievement and only subsequent events would prove the error in this leniency. The Ottomans deserved their victory; it was just unfortunate for them that the fruits of this success were not gathered. For the Russians and the Tsar it was a fortunate escape from a dreadful crisis, which not only could have easily changed the course of history completely, but also had dire consequences for the future of Peter the Great's dynasty. Tsar Peter had been humbled in the Balkans but managed to escape a hopeless situation relatively cheaply. The war with Sweden would now take a lot longer, but he went on to complete this victory, which would secure Russia's position as a Great Power.

Appendix I: The Response to the Ottoman Declaration of War[1]

This letter was sent by Tsar Peter to the Ottomans after the declaration of war, to claim it was not his fault and to set out his position.

We wrote twice to your Highness, namely, first, the 28th of July, and secondly, the 29th of October, of the last year, that according to intercepted Letters, and by the long Adobe of the King of Sweden in your Territiories, it was to be feared that that Price and his Adherents, with the Cossacks, Rebels to us, and to the King of Poland, our Ally; would by Means of the trayterous Palatine of Kiow, and others, who finding Refuge in your Territories, endeavours to engage your Highness in a War; for which Reason we desired that your Highness would Cause his Swedish Majesty forthwith to depart your Territories, and return into his own; offering him a free Passage through our Armies, under a Guard of 4000 Tartars, and 5000 Turks, in case your Highness should think it proper, for his greater Security: This is what our Ambassador was charged to propose to you; and his Polish Majesty having likewise consented to it, we were bound to answer for the said free passage.

Moreover, We declared, that in case your Highness would grant a more numerous Guard to the King of Sweden, and conduct him into Poland by force of Arms. This would be looked upon us, and by his Polish Majesty, that your Highness had a mind to break the Peace of Carlowitz, and that we should be obliged to oppose the same to the utmost of our Power, by Virtue of the Alliance, whereby we are mutually bound to assist each other.

We are not the violators of that Peace, but would religiously observe it on our Part, to prevent the Effusion of Human Blood; God will surely revenge it upon the Fomentor of the War, and Violator of the most Solemn Treaties: And should the King of Sweden offer to return into his Dominions by any other Way than has

---

[1]   A British officer in the service of the Czar, *An impartial History of the life and actions of Peter Alexowitz, the present Czar of Muscovy*, 1723, pp 320–323.

been proposed to him, under Colour of greater Security, we shall look upon that Proceeding as an open Violation of the Peace.

We have not yet received any Answer from your Highness, to our former Letters, nor from our Ambassador, to let us know whether he delivered them to your Highness, and whether he had any Answer or not: But on the Contrary, we have received certain Advice, from several Places, that our Ambassador has been arrested, that the War against us has been resolved upon at Constantinople, and Orders are given for forming an Army at Bender; and that the Tartars who are ready to conduct the King of Sweden, are ordered to enter Poland by Force of Arms; wherefore we thought fit to write this Letter to your Highness, to exhort you once more to answer our former Letters, and to let us know whether you intend to observe the Treaty prolonged with us last Year, for 30 Years, confirmed with several Oaths, made before the Judge of all our Actions, or to violate it, without the least Occasion on our Part given.

We also declare, that in case we receive no Answer touching your Intention to preserve the Peace, and that your Highness continues your Military Preparations, to conduct the King of Sweden through Poland, with a powerful Army, we shall look upon this as an open Violation of the Truce; and calling God to our Assistance, shall provide for our own Safety, and endeavour to repulse our Enemies with the Army we have sent upon the Frontier.

In the meanwhile, if the Rapture of the Peace be attended with the Effusion of Human Blood, we declare, before God and Man, that it will not be our Fault, but that we shall be forced to it. We likewise take God to Witness, that it was never our Intention to break the Truce, but to observe it religiously as we promised, wherefore, without Trusting in any vain Immagination, but only in the supreme Judge, we hope, he will defend us against all Disturbers of the Peace and Violators of Oaths.

We expect therefore, an Answer to these Presents, and in case none comes, we shall look upon it, as a Breach of the Peace; But if we see by your Highnesses Answer that your intention is to let us alone, and inviolably to maintain the Peace with us, (the King of Sweden being sent back. Without its being in any wise infringed) all our Umbrage will Cease.

And as our Army is advancing towards the Frontiers, without committing any Act of Hostility, the Rupture cannot be attributed to us; the less because, if the Satisfaction that is required be given us, our Troops shall forthwith withdraw from your Neighbourhood, and we will inviolably maintain the Truce, with your Highness: We wish your Highness perfect Health.

Given at Petersburgh, the 16th of January, 1711

Signed, Peter

Appendix II: The Moldavian Manifesto[1]

A manifesto calling on the Moldavians and other Christians to join the war against the Ottomans.

To the Right Reverend the Grecian Bishop of the Cathedral of Soczowa, the Illustrious and Potent Generals, and their Forces; together with all the other Subjects of Moldavia, Greetings.

WHEREAS the Enemies of the Holy Cross, in the Time of our Ancestors, did long oppress our People; and acting like Ravenous Wolves, thirsting after Innocent Christian Blood, though in Sheeps Cloathing, they reduced our Country under their Jurisdiction, and that of their False Prophet Mahomet; and constrained the then Hospodar to swear Fidelity to them, upon this Condition however, That the Lands of Moldavia should be liable to no other Tribute, besides the sending Yearly to Constantinople 4000 Ducats, 40 Horses, and 34 Falcons. But the Turks, instead of performing the Treaty which was concluded for that End did afterwards demolish our Castles, and caused the whole Country of Moldavia to be laid Waste by the Tartars, upon frivolous Pretences; and the Nobility and others of Distinction, of both Sexes, to be carried away into Captivity: They endeavoured, by Tortures, to constrain the former Hospodars, and their Ladies and Families, to embrace the Ottoman Faith. You cannot but be sensible, that they design at present to act the same Tragedy: But God's Mercy, towards us is visible, in hiving animated the Czar of Muscovy to appear in the Field with a Victorious Army, in order to rescue us, and other Christian Nations, from the Tyranny of the Infidels. 'Tis therefore necessary, to the effecting our Deliverance, that the Forces of this Country should march with all possible Diligence to the Danube, and oppose the intended Invasion of the Tartars; and the rather, because part of the Forces of his Czarish Majesty is arrived near Bender, and the rest of the Christian Army are going to pass the Bridge which we have built over the Danube with great

---

1   H. Rhodes (printer), *The Present State of Europe: or, the Historical and Political Monthly Mercury*, Volume XXII, 1711, p. 253.

Difficulty. For this Reason, the Czar has exhorted us, and others, that bear the Name of Christians to join his Majesty, who has already taken into his Pay 10000 of our Men, and committed the Money to my Custody: That Monarch promises, among other Things, to restore to this Country, such Fortresses as formerly belonged to us, and shall be re-taken from the Turks. We have therefore resolved, that if for the Future any of the Subjects of Moldavia take part with the Ottomans, they shall be publickly excommunicated, cursed, and deprived of the communion of the Saints –their Goods confiscated, and their Persons punished with Death: Therefore I conjure you, as you render your own Welfare, to follow our Steps, the sooner, the better, and to join the Czar's Army for whoever does not appear there before the 15th of June, shall incur the above mentioned Penalties.

Signed,

DEMETRIUS CANTIMAR,
Duke of MOLDAVIA

Appendix III: The Articles of Peace[1]

The articles of peace agreed on at the end of the active part of the campaign were as follows:

The Ground and Reasons of this authentick Writing is, That by the Grace of God the victorious Musselman Army having, by surrounding and shutting up the Czar of *Muscovy* with his whole Army in the Neighbourhood of the River *Pruth*, brought him into Straits, he himself desired Peace; and on the Instances of the said Czar, a Treaty and Articles were settled and concluded in the following manner.

1. That he shall restore the Fortress of *Asoph*, in the Condition wherein he formerly took it, with its Territories and Districts.

2. That *Taiganrog, Kamenki*, and the new Fort built on the further side of the River *Saman*, shall be totally demolished; the Cannon and Ammunition of War in the Fortress *Kamenki* or *Kaminieck*, to be left therein to the illustrious Porte, and no new Fort to be ever built in the same place.

3. That the Czar shall not concern himself with the *Pollacks*, nor with the *Cossacks* their Dependants, named *Barabasci* and *Potcali*; nor with the Dependants of the most successful Han *Doulet Gherai*; but shall leave them in their former Condition, and withdraw all his Forces out of those Countries.

4. That Mercants may come by Land into the well-guarded Dominions with their Merchandizes; but no Person shall be permitted to reside at the illustrious Porte in the Quality of Ambassador.

5. That all Musselmen, who formerly or in this War have been taken, and are Slaves in the hands of the Muscovites, shall be restored to Liberty.

---

1   Darby, pp. 126–128.

6. That the King of Sweden having taken Sanctuary under the Wings of the powerful Protection of the illustrious Porte, shall have free and safe Passage, without being in any manner hindered or stopped by the Muscovites; and in case they can come to a good Understanding together, and have a mind to make a Peace, it may in consequence be treated between them.

7. And for the future no Damage nor Injury shall be done by the Porte to the Muscovites; in like manner these last shall do no wrong to the former, or their Subjects or Dependants.

Wherefore the immense Royal Goodness of my most powerful and gracious Emperor and Lord is besought to be pleased to ratify the foregoing Articles, and to overlook the past ill Behaviour of the Czar.

Thus, and in the fore-mentioned manner, by virtue of the full Power to me given in this present Treaty made and delivered, we shall therefore confer about the Hostages given by the said Czar, for performance of the Articles contained in the said Instruments. Likewise the Treaties of Peace, named *Temeruki*, shall be mutually exchanged; after which his Army shall march off free the direct way to their own Country, without any Hindrance either by the victorious Army, by the *Tartars*, or others. The foregoing Articles shall of course be executed, and the Capitulation mutually exchanged; and we will immediately give Permission to the two Hostages to return home, that are in the victorious Army, namely, the chiefest among the Nobility of the Nation of the Messiah, his Privy Chancellor Baron *Peter Shaphirof*, and the Grandson of *Czeremet Michael Boris* (whose Ends be happy) after every Point shall have been performed. In Testimony of what is agreed, is this present Writing signed in the fore said Camp the 6th of the Month *Gemaiel Achir*, of the Year 1123 (or 21st of July, 1711).

Colour Plate Commentaries

Illustrations by Maksim Borisov, assisted by Boris Megorsky

PLATE A
Russian Army: Artillery and Command

In the centre is the Russian Tsar Peter as he may have appeared at the battle. He is depicted in clothing items he is known to have worn in the period 1709 and 1710, some of these have survived to this day. Peter was over two metres (6 feet) tall, hence his size compared to the others portrayed, and an active commander, hence he has taken off his coat. On the right is a senior officer of the army. He too has removed his coat in the Balkan heat and also his wig, which was commonly worn by the social elites of the period. The figure on the left is an artilleryman, once again without his coat. He is carrying both a cannonball and grapeshot. Russian guns were double loaded this way during the action to keep the Ottomans away. In the background of this plate are some *chevaux-de-fries* defences. These were constructed by pikes which had been cut down prior to the campaign for this purpose, and could be quickly constructed to provide defences.

PLATE B
Russian Army: Cavalry

Russian cavalry were regular units and uniformed, but there was no standard colour scheme. Individual units used different schemes and these could change over time, a unit did not have to have the same scheme when it received a new uniform. Overall the dress of the cavalry was similar to that which was popular at the time in Europe generally. Normally the coat was worn as depicted on the left hand and middle figures. It was extremely hot in the 1711 campaign so many would have removed the coat and fought in their vests, the figure on the right has done this. This figure is based on a partial description of the Kropotov Horse Grenadiers in 1711. This source only says that the breeches were leather and they had 'caps'. It is common that few details are know about Russian uniforms at this time and none are known about the 'cap' or indeed coat that this unit would have wore. It is likely, however, that the 'cap' would be of the mitre type and these were often covered, as shown, when on campaign. Dragoon regiments officially could wear two styles of headwear: the tricorn hat that was common in the period, and the *karpus* or *kartuz* cap, a very popular headwear for the Russian army. It had flaps to cover the ears and back of the head, and a front flap that could turn up or down like a visor.

The figure in the middle is based on a description of the Novgorodski Dragoons in 1710 with the front flap down as a visor, probably a popular choice in the sweltering heat of the 1711 campaign. This could also account for the hat worn by the figure on the left. The standard tricorn hat could be worn with the flaps unpinned and thus provide better protection from rain, and in 1711 from the sun. This illustration is based on a 1712 depiction of a soldier and the figure is dressed in the most common coat colour scheme, green with red cuffs and lining.

PLATE C
Russian Army: Infantry: Command and Grenadiers
In this plate, from left to right are an officer, a grenadier and a sergeant. As with the rest of the Russian army their dress was similar to that worn by most European armies of the time. The officer is fighting without his coat and covering his mouth from the clouds of dust from battle. The lace on the waistcoat and gorget indicate that he is an officer of the Guards. Officers of other units did not have gorgets at this time. The grenadier is member of the regiment of grenadiers originally raised from Hallart's division of the army. This is often called the 'Bils' grenadiers but was commanded by General Bon in 1711. They wore blue coats, but little else is known about their uniform at this time. The hat is based on a surviving grenadier cap and is speculative as there is no information. It is possible that foot grenadiers wore mitre type caps similar to those worn by the horse grenadiers. It is unlikely that the formal wear that is depicted in this illustration was common when actually on campaign.

The final figure on the right is a sergeant of the Butyrski Regiment. His dress is conventional for the era, but not his armament. Non-commissioned officers (NCOs) were often armed with halberds as shown, but not commonly with a pistol as well. In the Russian army of the time the pikemen were issued with a pistol as a secondary weapon. For the 1711 campaign the pikemen were rearmed as musketeers and their pistols given to the NCOs.

PLATE D
Russian Army: Infantry
Ordinary Russian infantry were issued with a coat, shoes, and boots. As with other figures the man on the left has removed his coat in the punishing weather the army suffered during the campaign. Most units were equipped with tricorn hats but these tended to lose their shape during a campaign and also could be turned down, perhaps as protection from the sun. This figure has turned down the flaps on his hat and his clothese are based on the uniform of the Koporski Regiment; he is wearing his shoes.

The figure on the right is wearing his boots, which were often more comfortable on campaign, and his coat. He also is wearing the other popular headwear in the army, the *karpus* or *kartuz* cap. The figure is based on what the Novgorodski infantry regiment was probably wearing during the campaign, a very dark green coat with red cuffs and lining along with a dark green and white cap. In addition to his musket this figure is also carrying a cut down pike. For this campaign the pikes were cut in two and the former pikemen rearmed with muskets. These halves of pikes were carried by the soldiers and used to construct *chevaux-de-fries* defences when threatened. This figure is also being plagued by locusts. General Bruce, a Scot fighting in the Russian army, noted that the army was plagued by swarms of locusts during the campaign which when combined with the heat, dust, and Ottoman threat made the campaign very unpleasant.

PLATE E
Russian Allies: Cossacks

Various Cossack groups were heavily involved in the Crimean and Kuban theatres. Cossacks are well known as light cavalry, but at this time also often fought on foot. Whether they fought on horseback or on foot the Cossacks all dressed similarly. The figure on the left, a mounted Cossack, is mainly distinguished from the figure on the right, a Cossack on foot, by their different footwear and headgear. The figure on the left has riding boots while that on the right does not have a horse and so wears shoes. Both kinds of hats were popular and other styles could be worn. The cap worn by the figure on the right was more typical of this era. The figures depict typical Cossack costume but as individuals would also wear other styles or clothing of the area. Only the poorest men fought exclusively on foot as they could not afford a horse, but all Cossacks could fight dismounted when needed. When on foot they relied on musket fire during combat. On horseback they still mainly relied on fire, pistol and carbine, but they could also utilise light lances and similar traditional weapons.

PLATE F
Russian Allies: Kalmyks, Moldavians and Walachians

The figure on the left is a Kalmyk. The Kalmyks had a good fighting reputation and were at the peak of their power. The army largely consisted of traditional horse archers and as such their main armament was their bow and arrows, which they could supplement with additional weapons. The figure has a horn ring for pulling the bow string and the distinctive forked musket rest that was used for sharpshooting. Their dress was traditional in nature and largely similar to that worn by the Mongolians. By this time other influences had begun to be felt, and so the figure's coat is fastened down the middle, rather than wrapped round in Mongolian style. A leather belt was traditional wear and as portrayed richly decorated in silver and niello. A Buddhist protective amulet is worn round the neck and like all Kalmyk men the figure has an earing in his left ear.

The figure on the right is a Moldavian or Walachian. The dress is typical of troops from the Balkans of the time but individuals could wear a variety of costumes or items popular in the wider region at the time. As with other contingents there would be little difference between individuals fighting on horseback and those fighting on foot. The primary weapons used would be firearms but more traditional weapons could also feature, such as the hatchet shown. The embroidery and fringe were popular in the Balkans.

PLATE G
Ottoman Allies: Exiled Polish Supporters of Stanisław Leszczyński and Charles XII of Sweden

The exiled supporters of the pro-Swedish faction in Poland in the Great Northern War would have looked like Polish soldiers of the then recent past. Pictured are a *pancerni* (on the left) and hussar (on the right), two of the main

Polish types of units. The third type was the *jazda lekka* (light cavalry), who are not pictured but would have been similar in appearance to the Cossack, Moldavian and Walachian figures on other plates. The *pancerni* derived their name from the metal armour these troops originally wore, typically chainmail and a helmet. By this period the use of armour was declining, although it was still used, and the figure has a mail coif and metal arm guard.

Hussars were the elite of the army but declining in numbers and importance. They continued to wear the fuller set of armour that this kind of warrior had traditionally worn but the great cost of this was one of the reasons for their declining numbers. A cloak of animal skin or fur was also often worn. In theory both types of cavalry, along with the *jazda lekka*, could continue to use the weapons of the past, lances, bows, etc., but in practice the Polish soldiers relied on swords, pistols and carbines in action. The wearing of armour, types of weapons used and exact costumes worn were all largely personal choice and so would vary greatly.

PLATE H

Ottoman Allies: Tatars and Exiled Swedes

The Swedes were the smallest allied group of the Ottomans but they were one of the underlying causes of the conflict. The Swedes dressed in Western-style uniforms of the period but with turnbacks on their coats as would become popular later in the century. The Swede depicted (on the left) is a member of the elite 'Drabant Corps'. This was the bodyguard unit of the Swedish King and had accompanied him into exile in 1709. As an elite unit they wore a richly decorated uniform topped off by a tricorn hat with gold lace. Other Swedish units wore similar uniforms but plainer.

The figure on the right is a Tatar from the Crimean Khanate, a close ally of the Ottomans and a formidable power in its own right. The bulk of the Tatar forces were light cavalry as the figure depicted here. This warrior is fairly traditionally equipped with bow and light lance but he could also possess pistols and carbines. Tatars could also wear elements of the costumes of the other irregular forces involved in this conflict such as the Cossacks, Kalmyks and Balkan light cavalry. Tatars of higher status could wear items of Ottoman style or from even further afield.

PLATE I

Ottoman Army: Infantry

Infantry were normally in the minority of Ottoman armies, but were an important component. Ottoman infantry were of two main types, the famous Janissaries and the Arnauts. The figure on the left is an Arnaut and the others are Janissaries. The Janissary corps was the feared elite regular formation of infantry of the Ottoman empire. The figure in the middle is wearing the more formal traditional dress associated with this esteemed corps. This included the distinctive headgear know as the *bork*, *bektasis* or ketche and long coat, the doloman. The figure is based on an illustration by Jean-baht Van Moore of an Ottoman delegation to Sweden. The Janissaries were a regular formation and so may have had coats and other apparel in uniform colours. There is little evidence that this was the case, but if it was it is likely that each unit of Janissary would have their own scheme, rather than a standard scheme across the whole body of troops. It does appear likely, however, that there was no uniformity and each individual chose the colours they wore. It is likely that the Janissaries did not always wear the costume when actively campaigning: ordinary Janissaries could and would wear more practical dress when on campaign, and the figure on the right gives an impression of what many would have looked like. The distinctive headgear has been rolled up and put with his backpack. Instead he is wearing a more comfortable and practical cap. However dressed, the Janissaries fought mainly with their long muskets and scimitars, although other weapons could be carried such as the hatchet pictured.

The army had units of musket-armed regulars which were raised by local dignitaries, officials, and other sources; the Janissaries were the household troops of the Sultan. The names of these units varied greatly depending on who raised them, the method of paying them, and various other factors. The figure on the left is an Arnaut, although this is a very inaccurate term: it is generic, used at the time to describe all of these troops. Because of this these troops would wear a variety of costumes, and depicted is a reasonably typical example. Many of these troops were raised in the Balkans and so could wear items common to that area. This figure is armed with a typical Balkan-style musket and is based on an illustration by Jean-baht Van Moore. As regular units it is possible that they could have worn some kind of uniform within each unit, but whether they did is unknown.

PLATE J
Ottoman Army: Cavalry

The bulk of Ottoman armies were cavalry, in particular those known as 'Sipahi'. The central figure is a *deli*. The *deli* were elite light cavalry who usually operated in small groups as a personal bodyguard for Ottoman officers and dignitaries, or as border patrols. In earlier times these troops had worn a distinctive costume with feathers or plumes on themselves and their shield, animal skins, and distinctive headgear. Yet by this time their dress was similar to that worn by other troops. The figure portrayed retains a few feathers, perhaps an echo of the past, and is also wearing an amulet or talisman. The figures on the left and right are Sipahi. Some of the Sipahi, the *kapu kulu*, were part of the Sultans household troops and were the elite regular cavalry of the army. Other Sipahi were recruited under a system similar to the feudal system and based on land grants. As with other Ottoman troops it is possible that the *kapu kulu* regular household Sipahi wore some kind of uniform items within their units. However it is more likely that, like the other Sipahi and troop types, they were not uniformed. In the past it was common for these troops to wear armour, usually mail and helmets, and to use traditional weapons such as bows, light lances and shields. Undoubtedly some individuals would continue to wear and use some of these, and the more traditional Sipahi from outside Europe tended to do so. Yet most now wore lighter clothing, although protective garments could be worn underneath. Various styles of turban had replaced helmets as the most common headgear, and similarly pistols and carbines had replaced more traditional armaments. The figure on the right depicts a more traditionally armed Sipahi, while the figure on the left is equipped with firearms.

PLATE K

Hilt of a broadsword found on Poltava battlefield. Exhibition of Azov Museum. (From the collection of Boris Megorsky)

PLATES L–P

Reenactment group 'Preobrazhensky Life Guard Regiment, 1709'. (From the collection of Boris Megorsky)

Select Bibliography

A British officer in the service of the Czar, An impartial History of the life and actions of Peter Alexowitz, the present Czar of Muscovy (London: Printed for W. Chetwood etc., 1723)

Agoston, G., 'Military Transformation in the Ottoman Empire and Russia, 1500–1800', *Kritika* 12, no. 2, 2011

Agoston, G., *Ottoman Warfare in Europe 1453–1826* in Black, J. (ed.), *European Warfare 1453–1815*. (London: Routledge, 1999)

Aksan, V. H., *Ottoman Wars 1700–1870: An Empire Besieged* (Harlow: Longmans, 2007)

Bancks, J., *The History of the life and reign of the Czar Peter the Great* (London: Printed for J. Hodges, at the Looking-Glass on London-Bridge, MDCCXL [1740])

Borekci, G. A., 'Contribution to the Military Revolution Debate: The Janissaries Use of Volley Fire During the Long Ottoman–Habsburg War of 1593–1606 and the Problem of Origins', *Acta Orientalia Academiae Scientiarum Hungricae*, vol. 59 (4), pp. 407–438, 2006

Bruce, P. H., *Memoirs of Peter Henry Bruce Esq. A Military Officer in the Service of Prussia, Russia and Great Britain* (Dublin: Printed by J. & R. Byrn etc., 1783)

Chandler, D., *The Art of Warfare in the Age of Marlborough* (Staplehurst: Spellmount, 1990)

Darby, J. (printer), *Complete history of the Turks: from their origin, in the year 755, to the year 1718*, 1719

Davies, B., *Empire and Military Revolution in Eastern Europe* (London: Continuum, 2011)

De Brasey, J. N., *Mémoires politiques, amusants et satyriques de messire J. N. D. B. C. db L., colonel du régiment de dragons de Casanski et brigadier des armées de S. M. Czarienne* (Veritopolie [i.e. Amsterdam]: Vrai [i.e. Roger], 1716)

Dorrell, N.A., *The Dawn of the Tsarist Empire* (Nottingham: Partizan Press, 2009)

Duffy, C., *Russia's Military Way to the West: origins and nature of russian military power 1700–1800* (London: Routledge & Kegan Paul, 1981)

Fabrice, E. F., *The Genuine Letters of Baron Fabricius* (London: Printed for T. Becket and P. A. Dehondt, at Tully's Head, in the Strand, M.DCC.LXI. [1761])

Goodwin. J., *Lords of the Horizons: A History of the Ottoman Empire* (London: Vintage, 1998)

Gush. G., *Renaissance Armies 1480–1650* (Cambridge: P. Stephens, 1975)

Hall, R. and Boeri, G., *Uniforms and Flags of the Imperial Austrian Army 1683–1720* (Pike and Shot Society, 2009)

Horsey, J. C. (ed.), *The Chronicles of an Old Campaigner, M. De La Colonie 1692–1717* (London: John Murray, 1904)

Juel, J., *Ambassade i Rusland, 1709–1711*, 1756

Kogălniceanu, M. and Niculcea, I., *Fragments tirés des chroniques moldaves et valaques pour servir il l'histoire de Pierre-le-grand, Charles XII, Démètre Cantimir et Constantin Brancovan (Fragments learned from Moldovan and Walachian chronicles to serve the stories of Peter the Great, Charles XII, Demetrius Cantemir and Constantine Brancovan)*, (Jassi: Au Bureau de la feuille communale, 1845)

Kurat, A. N., *The Despatches of Sir Robert Sutton, Ambassador in Constantinople (1710–1714)* (London: The Royal Historical Society, 1953)

La Motraye, A. de, *A. de La Motraye's Travels Through Europe, Asia, and Into Parts of Africa* (London : Printed for the author, in the Year MDCCXXIII. [1723])

Marsigli, L. F., *L'Etat Militaire de l'Empire Ottoman* (La Haye: N.p., 1732)

Massie, R. M., *Peter the Great: His Life and World* (London: Gollancz, 1981)

Motley, J., *The History of the Life of Peter I Emperor of Russia* (London : printed for J. Read, in White-Fryars, M.DCC.XL. [1740])

Murphey, R., *Ottoman Warfare, 1500–1700* (London: Routledge, 1999)

Nosworthy, B., *The Anatomy of Victory: Battle Tactics, 1689–1763* (New York: Hippocrene, 1992)

Perry, J., *The State of Russia, Under the Present Czar* (London : Printed for Benjamin Tooke, 1716)

Peter I, Tsar of Russia, *Journal de Pierre le Grand* (Stockholm: N.p., 1774)

Poniatowski, S., *Remarks on M. de Voltaire's History of Charles XII, King of Sweden* (London: Printed for J. Brindley, Bookseller to his Royal Highness the Prince of Wales etc., 1741)

Rhodes, H. (printer), *The Present State of Europe: or, the Historical and Political Monthly Mercury, Volume XXII*, 1711

Ricault, P., *The History of the Present State of the Ottoman Empire* (London : Printed for R. Clavell, J. Robinson and A. Churchill, in St. Paul's Church-Yard, and Avemary-Lane, 1686)

О.Г. Санин (O. G. Sanin), *Крымское ханство в Русско–Турецкая Война 1710–11 года (The Crimean Khanate in the Russian–Turkish War of 1710–11),* 2000

Sefere, H. O., *Prut Seferinde Lojistik ve Organizasyon (Prut Campaign, Logistics and Organization)* (place and publisher unknown, 2006)

Б.П. Шереметева (B. P. Sheremetev), *Военно-походный журнал фельдмаршала графа Б.П. Шереметева 1711 и 1712 (Military-marching Journal of Field Marshal Count BP Sheremetev 1711 and 1712),* 1898

А. Б. Широкорад (A. B. Shirokorad), *Русско–Турецкая Война 1710–1713 (The Russian–Turkish War 1710–1713),* 2000

Uyar, M. and Erickson, E. J., *A Military History of the Ottomans: From Osman to Atatürk* (Santa Barbara, Ca: Praeger Security International, 2009)

В. В. Звегинцов (V. V. Zvegintsov), *Русская Армия. Часть 1-я. 1700–1763гг. (The Russian Army: Part 1 1700–1763),* 1967